Taxcafe.co.uk Tax Guides

Tax Planning for Non-Residents & Non Doms 2017/18

Including all Tax Changes from the March 2017 Budget

By Nick Braun PhD

Important Legal Notices:

Taxcafe®
TAX GUIDE - 'Tax Planning for Non-Residents & Non Doms'

Published by:
Taxcafe UK Limited
67 Milton Road
Kirkcaldy
KY1 1TL
Tel: (0044) 01592 560081

2nd Edition, March 2017

ISBN: 978-1-911020-14-1

Disclaimer
Before reading or relying on the content of this tax guide please read the disclaimer.

Pay Less Tax!

...with help from Taxcafe's unique tax guides

All products available online at

www.taxcafe.co.uk

Popular Taxcafe titles include:

- *How to Save Property Tax*
- *Using a Property Company to Save Tax*
- *How to Save Inheritance Tax*
- *Landlord Interest*
- *Salary versus Dividends*
- *Using a Company to Save Tax*
- *Small Business Tax Saving Tactics*
- *Keeping it Simple: Small Business Bookkeeping, Tax & VAT*
- *Tax Planning for Non-Residents & Non Doms*
- *Tax Saving Tactics for Salary Earners*
- *Pension Magic*
- *Isle of Man Tax Saving Guide*
- *Tax-Free Capital Gains*
- *How to Save Tax*

Disclaimer

1. This guide is intended as **general guidance** only and does NOT constitute accountancy, tax, investment or other professional advice.

2. The author and Taxcafe UK Limited make no representations or warranties with respect to the accuracy or completeness of this publication and cannot accept any responsibility or liability for any loss or risk, personal or otherwise, which may arise, directly or indirectly, from reliance on information contained in this publication.

3. Please note that tax legislation, the law and practices by Government and regulatory authorities (e.g. HM Revenue & Customs) are constantly changing. We therefore recommend that for accountancy, tax, investment or other professional advice, you consult a suitably qualified accountant, tax adviser, financial adviser, or other professional adviser.

4. Please also note that your personal circumstances may vary from the general examples given in this guide and your professional adviser will be able to give specific advice based on your personal circumstances.

5. Any references to 'tax' or 'taxation', unless the contrary is expressly stated, refer to UK taxation only.

6. All persons described in the examples in this guide are entirely fictional. Any similarities to actual persons, living or dead, or to fictional characters created by any other author, are entirely coincidental.

About the Author & Taxcafe

Dr Nick Braun founded Taxcafe in 1999, along with his partner Aileen Smith. As the driving force behind the company, they aim to provide affordable plain-English tax information for private individuals, business owners and professional advisors.

Over the past 16 years Taxcafe has become one of the best-known tax publishers in the UK and has won several prestigious business awards.

Nick has been a specialist tax writer since 1989, first in South Africa, where he edited the monthly *Tax Breaks* publication, and since 1999 in the UK, where he has authored several tax books including *Small Business Tax Saving Tactics* and *Pension Magic*.

Nick also has a PhD in economics from the University of Glasgow, where he was awarded the prestigious William Glen scholarship and later became a Research Fellow.

Contents

Introduction

This guide will show you how to reduce your tax bill if you are non-UK resident or non-domiciled.

We kick off in Part 1 with the new Statutory Residence Test which will help you determine whether you are UK resident or non-resident for tax purposes. The test replaces HMRC's old (and somewhat vague) guidance.

The test has three components:

- **The automatic overseas tests.** You can become automatically *non-resident* if you spend few enough days in the UK during the tax year (15 or 45 depending on your circumstances) or by working overseas.

- **The automatic UK tests.** If you do not satisfy any of the automatic overseas tests you move on to the automatic UK tests. You will be automatically UK *resident* if you spend too much time in the UK during the tax year (more than 182 days), or if you have a home in the UK or work in the UK for a certain length of time.

- **The sufficient ties test.** If you do not meet any of the automatic overseas or UK tests you use the sufficient ties test to determine your residence status. This test takes account of your UK ties (e.g. whether you have accommodation in the UK or work here) and the number of days you spend in the country. The more ties you have, the more difficult it is to become non-UK resident.

When you first leave the UK you may qualify for *split-year treatment* which means the tax year will be split into a UK part (when you will be taxed as a UK resident) and an overseas part (when you will be taxed as non-resident). New rules govern who qualifies for this special tax treatment and these are explained in detail.

The Statutory Residence Test is supposed to be simple but can get quite complicated, so lots of examples are used to explain how it works in practice and what you have to do to achieve your desired residence status.

Alongside the Statutory Residence Test, anti-avoidance rules have been introduced to prevent individuals leaving the country for a short space of time (five years or less) and realizing tax-free capital gains. The rules also clamp down on individuals who wish to pay themselves tax-free dividends and certain other types of income after becoming non-resident. These rules are also explained in detail.

Income Tax Planning

In Part 2 we move on to income tax planning for non-UK residents. There are nine different chapters that show you how to minimise the tax payable on different types of income after becoming non-resident, including:

- Rental income
- Dividend income
- Interest income
- Pension income, and
- Employment income

The chapter on rental income explains how property investors are taxed when they become non-resident, how the Non-Resident Landlord Scheme operates and how you can minimize your income tax after becoming non-resident.

The chapter on dividends explains how non-residents can pay themselves tax-free dividends. However, this exemption comes at a price and you could end up paying more tax on your other UK income, for example your rental income. If you're not careful you could also end up paying more tax on your dividends in the country you move to than you would as a UK resident.

In the chapter on interest income we look at how non-residents can enjoy tax-free interest (and again the potential danger for those with other types of UK income). We also look at how various double tax treaties can limit the amount of tax HMRC can levy on your income.

Retiring Abroad & Working Abroad

The chapter on pensions is pretty detailed and should be of interest to anyone thinking of retiring abroad. It covers Government pensions, private pensions and state pensions which are all taxed differently if you are non-resident.

For example, under many tax treaties UK occupational pensions and other private pensions are exempt from UK tax, i.e. they are only taxed in the overseas country where you live. Having your UK pension taxed overseas only could be extremely tax efficient if the country you move to has lower tax rates than the UK.

We also take a look at why it may be worth making voluntary national insurance contributions if you live overseas so that you can qualify for a bigger state pension and why it may be worth taking your tax-free pension lump sum before you leave the UK to avoid paying tax on it overseas.

There is also a separate chapter on the pros and cons of transferring your pension abroad to a QROPS. Some of these transfers will be hammered by a new 25% tax announced in the March 2017 Budget.

Many individuals go abroad to work so this part of the guide also contains a detailed chapter on employment income, including how to avoid UK income tax if you work in the UK, how to enjoy tax-free relocation costs and whether you will pay UK national insurance or social security contributions in another country.

We end with a chapter covering how income is taxed in other countries, including tax havens, countries with top tax rates of 20% or less, countries that are popular with UK expats and countries that do not tax foreign income (i.e. UK income).

Capital Gains Tax Planning

Part 3 covers capital gains tax planning.

The first chapter covers UK capital gains tax, including:

- The rules for temporary non-residents
- How business assets are taxed
- The new tax (from April 2015) on non-residents who sell UK residential property
- Why it may be worth selling assets before you become non-resident
- How to enjoy an unlimited capital gains tax exemption on your UK home if you work overseas

The second chapter covers overseas capital gains tax, including a list of countries that do not tax capital gains and how capital gains are taxed in various countries popular with UK expats.

Tax Saving Tactics for Non-Doms

In Part 4 the focus is taxpayers who are non-UK domiciled. Non doms can choose to be taxed on the remittance basis which means they only pay tax on their overseas income and capital gains when the money is brought into the UK.

However, making a claim to pay tax on the remittance basis can be very costly. Not only will you lose your personal allowance and annual capital gains tax exemption, you may also have to pay the £30,000 or £60,000 remittance basis charge if you've been living in the UK for a certain length of time.

The first chapter in this part of the guide explains how your domicile is decided and what you need to do to lose your UK domicile or avoid acquiring a UK domicile if you are currently non-domiciled.

In the chapters that follow we examine:

- The new rule (from 6 April 2017) that makes you deemed UK domiciled for all tax purposes once you've been UK resident for 15 years

- The tax benefits of offshore trusts and how they can still be used by non doms to roll up family wealth tax free

- Concessions that allow non-domiciled individuals with small amounts of overseas income to benefit from the remittance basis without paying any penalty

- When it does and does not make sense to claim the remittance basis

- How to avoid the £30,000/£60,000 remittance basis charge

- The rules for non-domiciled employees who use dual contracts to avoid UK income tax

- Tax-free remittances you can make, including the new Business Investment Relief for those investing in UK companies

- Inheritance tax planning, including using excluded property trusts and new rules to tax UK residential property held in offshore companies.

I hope you enjoy reading the guide and find it useful!

Using This Guide & Limitations

This guide was created to explain, in plain English, how individuals are taxed when they are non-UK resident and non-UK domiciled. Please note that it is NOT supposed to be a do-it-yourself ('DIY') tax planning tool. If you are planning to take any action based on the contents, I strongly recommend that you obtain professional advice.

Although the guide covers a fair amount of ground, it does not cover every possible scenario and angle. The subject is simply too large. Furthermore, individuals come in many different shapes and sizes, so it's possible that the information contained in this guide will not be relevant to your circumstances.

There are also non-tax factors that have to be considered and these may be as important or more important than the tax issues.

Tax rates and tax laws (including HMRC's interpretation of those laws) are continually changing. The reader must bear this in mind when reading the chapters that follow.

For all of these reasons, it is vital that you obtain professional advice before taking any action based on the information contained in this publication. The author and Taxcafe UK Ltd cannot accept any responsibility for any loss which may arise as a consequence of any action taken, or any decision to refrain from action taken, as a result of reading this guide.

Part 1

The Statutory Residence Test

Chapter 1

The Old Rules

Before the introduction of the Statutory Residence Test your residence status for tax purposes depended largely on HMRC guidance derived from case law. This guidance was published in a document known as IR20 (later HMRC6).

Although IR20 was not legally binding, many tax advisors relied heavily on its content when advising their clients.

IR20 provided two main ways of becoming non-resident:

- Going abroad under a full-time contract of employment
- Leaving the UK permanently or indefinitely

Leaving the UK to work full-time abroad was generally not controversial. To become non-resident your absence from the UK and your overseas job had to last for at least one whole tax year and you had to keep your UK visits within certain limits:

- Less than 183 in any tax year, and
- Less than 91 days per tax year on average

Leaving the UK Permanently

Becoming non-resident the second way – leaving the UK permanently or indefinitely – became the main problem area following some high-profile court cases.

According to IR20, if you went abroad permanently or indefinitely (or for a period of three years or more) you were generally treated as non-UK resident if your UK visits averaged 90 days or less per year. Many taxpayers relied heavily on day counting alone to remain non-resident.

However, HMRC felt that some taxpayers were 'fiddling the system' – living outside the UK for most of the year BUT maintaining strong personal and social ties here.

The Gaines-Cooper Case

It all came to a head with the Supreme Court case involving HMRC and Robert Gaines-Cooper. Robert Gaines-Cooper was a wealthy businessman who went to live in the Seychelles in 1976. He argued that he kept his UK visits within the limits and was therefore non-resident.

However, HMRC argued that its guidance also required taxpayers to make a distinct break from the UK by severing their ties – day counting alone was not enough.

Robert Gaines-Cooper's wife and child lived in the UK and he owned a substantial house here plus a collection of classic cars and paintings. Thus HMRC argued that he had not made a clean break from the UK and was therefore UK resident.

Although expert witnesses argued that HMRC was performing a u-turn, the court sided with the taxman and found that Robert Gaines-Cooper had not left the UK permanently or indefinitely and was UK resident for tax purposes.

The Statutory Residence Test

This case and others created a huge amount of uncertainty. It became virtually impossible for many taxpayers to know for sure whether they were UK resident or non-resident.

Thus a decision was made to introduce a new Statutory Residence Test which would provide a clear-cut formula to allow taxpayers to determine their residence status.

After a lengthy period of consultation and a huge amount of tweaking the test finally arrived and has been in operation since 6 April 2013 (i.e. the start of the 2013/14 tax year).

Although the new test provides greater certainty for some taxpayers it can get quite complex and some taxpayers will struggle to apply it in practice.

Chapter 2

Introduction to the Statutory Residence Test

This chapter contains a brief overview of the Statutory Residence Test. The test tells you whether you are UK resident or non-resident for tax purposes.

It's all about the number of days you spend in the UK – the more days you spend here, the harder it is to become non-resident.

Another important factor is work. If you get a full-time job overseas, it is relatively easy to become non-resident.

If you wish to 'push the envelope' and increase the number of days you spend in the UK, you may have to reduce your UK ties in order to demonstrate that you have genuinely left the country.

The test applies on a tax year by tax year basis. In other words, if you are non-resident this year, that doesn't mean you are automatically non-resident next year.

The devil is in the detail and in the chapters that follow we will take a closer look at each component of the test and what terms like "days", "home" and "work" mean in practice.

It is also important to point out that the Statutory Residence Test only decides your residence position under UK law. If the UK and the country you move to both treat you as resident at the same time, you may have to rely on the tie-breaker clause in the relevant double tax treaty, if there is one.

In other words, you could be UK resident under the Statutory Residence Test but non-resident under a double tax treaty.

Leavers and Arrivers

The Statutory Residence Test distinguishes between two groups of individuals, namely those who were:

- UK resident in *any* of the previous 3 tax years ("leavers")

- UK resident in *none* of the previous 3 tax years ("arrivers")

If you were UK resident in *any* of the previous three tax years you will find it harder to become non-resident than someone who was not.

Automatic Overseas Tests

You start with the automatic overseas tests. You will be automatically *non-resident* for the tax year if you meet *any* of the following tests:

- You spend fewer than 16 days in the UK during the tax year. This test is used if you were UK resident in *any* of the previous 3 tax years.

- You spend fewer than 46 days in the UK during the tax year. This test is used if you were UK resident in *none* of the previous three tax years.

- If you work sufficient hours overseas (generally 35 hours or more per week on average) without a significant break, and during the tax year:

    ➤ You spend fewer than 91 days in the UK, and
    ➤ You spend fewer than 31 days working in the UK (a work day means more than three hours work).

If you do not meet any of these automatic overseas tests, you should move onto the 'automatic UK tests'.

Automatic UK Tests

You will be automatically *UK resident* for the tax year if you meet *any* of the following tests:

- You spend 183 days or more in the UK during the tax year.

- You have a home in the UK and are present in that home on 30 or more days during the tax year. This test only applies if you do not have an overseas home or, if you do have an overseas home, you are present in that home on fewer than 30 days during the tax year.

- You work full time in the UK for any period of 365 days (all or part of which falls into the tax year) with no significant break.

If any of the automatic UK tests apply to you for a particular tax year and none of the automatic overseas tests apply, you are UK resident for tax purposes for that tax year.

If you do not meet any of the automatic overseas tests and do not meet any of the automatic UK tests you have to use the sufficient ties test to determine your residence status for the tax year.

Sufficient Ties Test

This test takes into account your UK ties and the number of days you spend in the UK. The more ties you have, the more likely it is that you will be UK resident for tax purposes:

- **Family tie** – your spouse (unless separated) or partner (if you are living together as husband and wife) or children under 18 (with some exceptions) are UK resident.

- **Accommodation tie** – you have a place to live in the UK that is available for a continuous period of 91 days or more during the tax year. You don't have to own the property but must spend at least one night there during the tax year to have an accommodation tie. If it is the home of a close relative, you must spend 16 or more nights there to have an accommodation tie.

- **Work tie** – you do more than three hours work a day in the UK for a total of at least 40 days. Includes employment and self-employment.

- **90-day tie** – you have spent more than 90 days in the UK in either or both of the previous two tax years.

- **Country tie** – the UK is the country in which you were present for the greatest number of days during the tax year. This tie only applies if you were UK resident in any of the previous three tax years.

These ties are then combined with days spent in the UK to determine your residence status.

The scoring is different for people who have recently left the UK (i.e. were UK resident in any of the previous three tax years) and those who have recently arrived (i.e. were not resident in any of the previous three tax years).

UK Resident in Any of Previous 3 Tax Years – Leavers

UK ties are combined with days spent in the UK as follows:

Days in UK	Residence status
Fewer than 16 days	Always non-resident
16 – 45 days	UK Resident if 4 or more ties
46 – 90 days	UK Resident if 3 or more ties
91 – 120 days	UK Resident if 2 or more ties
121-182 days	UK Resident if 1 or more ties
183 days or more	Always UK resident

Not Resident in All 3 Previous Tax Years – Arrivers

UK ties are combined with days spent in the UK as follows:

Days in UK	Resident Status
Fewer than 16 days	Always non-resident
16 – 45 days	Always non-resident
46 – 90 days	UK resident if all 4 ties
91 – 120 days	UK resident if 3 or more ties
121-182 days	UK resident if 2 or more ties
183 days or more	Always UK resident

International Transport Workers

The third automatic overseas test (the one that can make you non-resident if you work abroad) does *not* apply if, at any time during the tax year, you have what's called a "relevant job" – i.e. you work on board aircraft, ships or in vehicles while they are crossing international boundaries – and at least six of the trips you make during the tax year are cross-border trips that begin in the UK, end in the UK or begin and end in the UK.

Similarly, the third automatic UK test (the one that makes you UK resident if you work here) does *not* apply to these workers.

Those affected must use the other tests to determine their residence status. Affected persons include pilots and cabin crew, cross channel ferry staff, mariners and lorry drivers where "substantially all" the trips they make are cross-border trips.

According to HMRC guidance you are likely to be considered to have a "relevant job" if 80% or more of your trips are cross-border trips.

Death during the Tax Year

There are different rules for people who die during the tax year. These rules are not covered in this tax guide.

Summary

The Statutory Residence Test will make it very easy for some people to become non-resident.

When you first leave the UK all you have to do is spend fewer than 16 days per tax year in the UK and you will definitely be non-resident.

After three tax years you can increase the amount of time you spend in the UK – as long as you spend fewer than 46 days per year in the country you will definitely be non-resident.

However, it becomes more complicated if you wish to spend more time in the UK.

Chapter 3

Days Spent in the UK

Because the Statutory Residence Test revolves around days spent in the UK, it is important to explain precisely what is meant by a "day spent in the UK".

You are treated as having spent a day in the UK if you are here at midnight.

Transit Days

Transit days can be ignored when counting the number of days you've spent in the UK.

A transit day is one where you travel through the UK from one country to another. To be counted as a transit day you must arrive in the UK as a passenger and leave the next day.

While you are in the UK you are not allowed to do anything substantially unrelated to your travel through the UK.

Example

Paul flies into Heathrow from Amsterdam on Thursday in order to catch a flight to New York that leaves the next day.

If Paul stays in his hotel room watching TV, the transit arrival day (Thursday) will not be counted as a day spent in the UK. The departure day (Friday) could count as a day spent in the UK if the deeming rule applies to Paul (see below).

If Paul meets up with some friends and goes out for dinner or has a business meeting with a UK colleague, the transit arrival day (Thursday) will be counted as a day spent in the UK. The departure day (Friday) may also count as a day spent in the UK if the deeming rule applies to Paul (see below).

HMRC is taking a tough stance with respect to what you can and cannot do when passing through the UK.

Example revised

Paul flies into Heathrow from Amsterdam on Thursday to catch a flight to New York leaving the next day. He intends to simply relax in his hotel but bumps into a work colleague at the airport. They go for coffee and talk about their families, holidays and other matters unrelated to work. That evening Paul looks at his colleague's photos on Facebook.

HMRC's view is that Paul's chance meeting with his colleague and his use of social media IS related to his transit through the UK because the meeting was unplanned and there was no discussion of work. Thus Paul's day of arrival (Thursday) will be treated as a transit day and will not count as a day spent in the UK for the purposes of the Statutory Residence Test.

If, however, Paul and his colleague also discuss work matters and, back at his hotel later that evening, Paul emails his boss about the meeting, in HMRC's eyes these activities are unrelated to his transit through the UK and his day of arrival (Thursday) may be treated as a day spent in the UK. If he works for more than three hours, the day will also count as a UK work day. Paul's departure day (Friday) may also count as a day spent in the UK if the deeming rule applies to him (see below).

Exceptional Circumstances

It may be possible to ignore certain days spent in the UK if you are here because of exceptional circumstances. The maximum number of days that can be ignored is 60.

Exceptional circumstances are usually events beyond your control that prevent you from leaving the UK. You must, however, leave as soon as possible.

Examples of exceptional circumstances are likely to include natural disasters, civil unrest and life-threatening illness or injury (including life-threatening illness or injury suffered by your spouse/partner or dependent children).

However, if you choose to come to the UK for medical treatment, this will not be treated as exceptional circumstances.

According to HMRC guidance, delayed or missed flights, train delays or cancellations or car breakdowns do not count as exceptional circumstances.

If you return to the UK because the Foreign and Commonwealth Office has advised against travel to a particular region, the days spent in the UK will be ignored, subject to the 60-day limit.

The Deeming Rule

The general rule is that, if you leave the UK before midnight, that day does not count as a day spent in the UK.

Arguably, this means that someone could rack up a large amount of time in the UK and remain non-resident by commuting from, say, the Isle of Man or France and leaving each day before midnight. To combat this, the test contains a 'deeming rule' – some days are counted even if you are not in the UK at midnight.

The deeming rule will only apply if you have:

- Been UK resident in any of the preceding three tax years
- At least three UK ties
- Been present in the UK on more than 30 days during the tax year without being present at the end of the day

If you meet all of these conditions the deeming rule applies. This means that, after the first 30 qualifying days, all subsequent days are treated as days that you spent in the UK.

Example

Wendy does not meet the automatic overseas tests or the automatic UK tests and therefore has to determine her residence status using the sufficient ties test.

She spent 35 days in the UK where she was present at midnight and was also present on 55 other days but left before the end of the day.

She was UK resident in the previous tax year and has three UK ties (see Chapter 6 for more on ties).

Because there are more than 30 days when she left before the end of the day, she has to use the deeming rule. This gives her a total of 60 days spent in the UK – the 35 days when she was present at midnight plus 25 other days (ignoring the first 30).

With 60 days spent in the UK and three UK ties Wendy will be UK resident under the sufficient ties test.

The 90 Day Tie

For the deeming rule to apply you must have three or more UK ties. One of the ties that has to be considered is the '90-day tie' which applies if you have spent more than 90 days in the UK in either of the previous two tax years.

However, when calculating if the 90-day limit has been exceeded the deeming rule does not apply, i.e. you only include days when you were present in the UK at the end of the day.

Example

Helga is trying to establish her residence status for the current tax year. During the current tax year there are 50 days when she was in the UK but not present at the end of the day. She was UK resident in the previous tax year and definitely has 2 UK ties. She wants to know if the 90-day tie also applies, in which case she will have three ties and the deeming rule will apply.

In the previous two tax years she was present in the UK as follows:

Year 1 – She was in the UK at the end of the day on 70 days and on another 50 days she left the UK before the end of the day.
Year 2 – She was in the UK at the end of the day on 60 days and on another 40 days she left the UK before the end of the day.

For the deeming rule, only the days when Helga was in the UK at midnight matter. In both years these days did not exceed 90, so Helga does not have a 90-day tie for the current tax year and the deeming rule will therefore not apply.

Non-Resident in Previous Three Tax Years

If you were UK resident in none of the previous three tax years you can visit the country for up to 45 days per tax year without becoming resident for tax purposes.

For these individuals, days when you are not present at the end of the day are not counted, so it may be possible for those who live within commuting distance to spend a significant amount of time in the UK without becoming UK resident for tax purposes.

Chapter 4

The Automatic Overseas Tests

When applying the Statutory Residence Test you start with the automatic overseas tests. You will be *non-resident* for the tax year if you pass *any* of the following tests:

- **First automatic overseas test**. You spend fewer than 16 days in the UK during the tax year. This test is only used if you were UK resident in any of the previous 3 tax years.

- **Second automatic overseas test**. You spend fewer than 46 days in the UK during the tax year. This test is only used if you were UK resident in none of the previous 3 tax years.

- **Third automatic overseas test.** You work sufficient hours overseas (generally 35 hours or more per week on average) without a significant break, and during the tax year:

    - You spend fewer than 91 days in the UK, and
    - You spend fewer than 31 days working in the UK (a work day means more than 3 hours work).

If you satisfy any of the above three tests, you will definitely be non-resident for the tax year in question and will not have to consider any other part of the Statutory Residence Test. The tests are different if you die during the tax year.

The First & Second Automatic Overseas Tests

The first and second automatic overseas tests are ideal for those who don't want to get into all the complexity of the Statutory Residence Test. Just keep the number of days you spend in the UK to a minimum (fewer than 16 or 46) and you will definitely be non-resident.

The first and second automatic overseas tests are suitable for those who leave the UK and intend to return for short holidays only.

Unfortunately, if you emigrated recently (i.e. you are a 'leaver'), you must spend fewer than 16 days per year in the UK if you wish to remain non-resident under the first automatic overseas test. Many would find such short visits untenable.

Once you have been non-resident for at least three tax years the number of days you can spend in the UK each year increases to 45.

If you want to spend more time in the UK you have to either work overseas (see below) or examine your UK ties (see Chapter 6).

Third Automatic Overseas Test – Overseas Work

If you work overseas you can potentially spend up to 90 days per year in the UK and automatically be treated as non-resident.

To qualify you must work "sufficient hours" overseas (generally 35 hours or more per week on average) without a significant break, and during the tax year:

- You must spend fewer than 91 days in the UK, and
- You must spend fewer than 31 days working in the UK (if you do more than three hours, it's a UK work day).

What is a significant break from overseas work?

If you have a significant break from overseas work you cannot use the overseas work test to be non-resident. Generally speaking, a significant break occurs if 31 days go by and you have not worked for more than three hours on any of those days.

Allowances are made for annual leave, sick leave and parental leave.

The 90 Day Limit

Remember the deeming rule whereby some days are counted even if you are not in the UK at midnight? The deeming rule does not apply to the limit on days spent in the UK under the third automatic overseas test.

Calculating Sufficient Hours

Fortunately you don't have to work for an average of 35 hours per week *every week* of the tax year. The taxman gives you credit for things like annual leave, sick leave, maternity leave and breaks between jobs.

Step 1 – Calculate Your Net Overseas Hours

Calculate the total number of hours you worked overseas during the tax year. Include all jobs and hours worked while self-employed. Ignore days worked in the UK for more than 3 hours.

Step 2 – Calculate Your Reference Period

Subtract the following days from 365:

- Disregarded days – days in which you do more than three hours work in the UK
- Gaps between employments – up to 15 days for each gap with an overall maximum of 30 per tax year. Does not apply to gaps between self-employed work
- Sick leave
- Annual leave and maternity or paternity leave, providing reasonable in the country in which you are working
- Non-working days embedded within your leave (e.g. weekends and public holidays). Only include these non-working days if they are preceded or followed by at least three days of leave

Step 3

Divide the number of days in your reference period by 7. Round down to the nearest whole number. If the answer is less than one, round it up to one.

Step 4

Divide your net overseas hours by the number obtained in Step 3.

If the answer is 35 hours or more, you have worked sufficient hours overseas for the purposes of the third automatic overseas test.

Example

Steve worked in France during the tax year and wants to know if he meets the third automatic overseas test. He worked for two French employers during the tax year.

His first job ran from 6 April to 23 August (20 weeks). He worked for eight hours per day on average, five days per week. During that time he took 9 days leave (with no embedded non-working days).

He then resigned and took a 30 day holiday travelling around Spain. Feeling refreshed, he started his second job in France, working from 23 September to 5 April (the last day of the tax year).

He worked for 8 hours per day on average, five days per week and took the following leave:

- *Five days to cover public holidays and a long weekend.*

- *10 days of annual leave, with two embedded non-working days (the Saturday and Sunday in the middle of the two weeks).*

- *Five days of sick leave, with no embedded non-working days.*

Step 1 – Net Overseas Hours

Employer 1:	
20 weeks x 5 days	*100 days*
Less: 9 days leave	*91 days*
8 hours per day	*728 hours*
Employer 2:	
28 weeks x 5 days	*140 days*
Less: 20 days leave	*120 days*
8 hours per day	*960 hours*
Total net overseas hours	*1,688 hours*

Step 2 –Reference Period

Subtract from 365 days:

- *Disregarded days*   *0 days*
- *Gaps between jobs*   *15 days (the maximum)*
- *Sick leave*   *5 days*
- *Annual leave*   *26 days (9 + 5 + 10 + 2 embedded)*

Reference period is 319 days.

Step 3

Divide reference period by 7 = 319/7 = 45.57 and round down to 45.

Step 4

Divide net overseas hours by the number obtained in Step 3:

1,688/45 = 37.5 hours

The cut-off is 35 hours, so Steve has worked sufficient overseas hours to be automatically non-UK resident for tax purposes.

What Is Work?

According to HMRC work takes its every day meaning. If you are an employee, work includes carrying out your duties. If you are self-employed work means time spent carry out your trade, profession or vocation. Voluntary work does not count.

When adding up time spent working you should include:

- Travel time if the cost would have been tax deductible if incurred by you, regardless of whether or not you worked during the journey
- Travel time spent working, regardless of whether the cost would have been tax deductible
- Training paid by your employer or tax deductible if self-employed
- Time spent serving notice away from work

Chapter 5

The Automatic UK Tests

If you do not satisfy any of the automatic overseas tests you move on to the 'automatic UK tests'. You will be automatically *UK resident* for the tax year if you meet *any* of the following tests:

- **First automatic UK test.** You spend 183 days or more in the UK during the tax year.

- **Second automatic UK test.** You have a home in the UK during the tax year and are present in that home on 30 or more days during the tax year. This test only applies if you do not have an overseas home or, if you do have an overseas home, you are present in that home on fewer than 30 days during the tax year.

- **Third automatic UK test.** You work in the UK for any period of 365 days (all or part of which falls into the tax year) with no significant break.

First Automatic UK Test

If you spend 183 days or more in the UK during the tax year you will be UK resident for that tax year.

Does this mean you can spend *almost* 183 days in the UK – perhaps even 182 days – and still be non-resident for tax purposes? The answer is yes but it may be very difficult, especially if you are a leaver (UK resident in any of the previous three tax years).

Firstly, you must not satisfy the other two automatic UK tests listed above. For example, if you have a UK home in which you are present for 30 days or more during the tax year (highly possible if you are spending almost half the year in the UK) it will be essential to also have an overseas home and spend at least 30 days in that home during the tax year.

Providing you do not satisfy any of the automatic UK tests your residence status will be determined using the sufficient ties test (see Chapter 6). This test allows you to spend over 120 days in the UK and still be non-UK resident if:

- You have no UK ties   Leavers
- You have one UK tie   Arrivers

It may be difficult, if not impossible, to spend almost half the year in the UK and have just one or no UK ties (e.g. no work tie and no accommodation tie).

In fact, if you've spent more than 90 days in the UK in either of the previous two tax years this itself counts as one UK tie. This will initially prevent many leavers from spending over 120 days in the UK while remaining non-resident.

Second Automatic UK Test

This test is designed to catch people who go abroad (perhaps for a long holiday) but still have a home in the UK.

You will meet this test if there is a period of 91 consecutive days (with at least 30 of those days falling into the tax year) when:

- You have a home in the UK in which you are present on at least 30 days during the tax year, and

- You have no overseas home or, if you do have an overseas home, you are present in that home on fewer than 30 days during the tax year.

You are 'present' at your home if you spend *any time* at the property, no matter how short the stay.

You can ignore any homes in which you are present on fewer than 30 days during the tax year. Thus if you have a home in the UK you can avoid becoming automatically UK resident by making sure you are physically present there on fewer than 30 days.

Alternatively, you can make sure you don't have a UK home by renting out your UK home or selling it as soon as possible after you go abroad.

You can also avoid becoming UK resident by making sure you have an overseas home throughout the tax year and are present in that home on 30 or more days during the tax year.

Example

Albert has lived in the UK all his life and has a home here. After retiring he decides to spend several years travelling around the world. During the current tax year he visits many countries without establishing a home in any of them.

He keeps his UK home and returns for occasional short visits. He is present in the property on 50 days during the tax year.

Because he has no overseas home and is present in his UK home on at least 30 days during the tax year he is UK resident under the second automatic UK test for the current tax year.

Example

Caroline has a home in the UK for the whole of the 2017/18 tax year and is present there on more than 30 days.

Caroline acquires an overseas home on 1 March 2018 and spends 30 days in it during the 2017/18 tax year. Although Caroline has an overseas home during the tax year and spent 30 days in it during the tax year she will still be UK resident.

This is because there is a period of at least 91 consecutive days (6 April 2017 to 28 February 2018) when she had a UK home (in which she spent sufficient time in 2017/18) but no overseas home.

Caroline is therefore resident in the UK for 2017/18 under the second automatic UK test.

More than One Home

If you have more than one home the test is applied to each home separately. If you have more than one home you could spend time in different homes and not be caught by this rule, as long as you spend fewer than 30 days in each home during the tax year.

Example

Aru has three UK homes. During the current tax year he is present in his home in London on 29 days, 29 days in his flat in Edinburgh and 29 days in his house in Brighton. Aru has been present in his UK homes on 87 days in total. However, because he was not present in any single home on at least 30 days he will not meet the second automatic UK test for the tax year under consideration.

What is a Home?

The Statutory Residence Test does not provide a concrete definition of "home" – it all depends on your personal circumstances and how you use a property. Here are some general pointers:

It is possible to have more than one home, either in one country or several countries.

Example

Rory's wife and children live in the UK but he does most of his work in Dublin. He flies to Ireland every Sunday evening and returns to the UK every Thursday night. In Dublin he lives in a rented flat. In the UK he lives with his family in a property he owns with his wife. Both properties are his homes.

A property can be your home even if you do not stay there continuously, for example if you move out for a while but your spouse and children still live there.

Example

Deryck's employer sends him to Hong Kong to work for three months. He stays in a hotel while he's there. His wife continues to live in their flat in

Edinburgh. Deryck returns to live with his wife in their Edinburgh flat after his secondment. The Edinburgh flat was Deryck's home throughout the period of his secondment.

A property can still be your home even if you move out temporarily but the property remains available.

Example

Anna has lived in a flat she owns in London for the last 10 years. Her father lives in Germany and is seriously ill so Anna moves there to look after him. Her London flat remains empty and available even though she hasn't returned to London since leaving the UK 10 months ago. Anna will have a home both in Germany and London.

A property is only your home if you use it as your home.

Example

Paul completed the purchase of a new house in Bristol on 1 March. Before moving his belongings in and staying there he carries out some renovation work and redecorates the property. He finally moves into the property on 15 August. The house only becomes Paul's home from 15 August onwards.

Similarly, a property that is purchased solely as an investment or that you inherit but never stay in will not be a home.

A property is not your home if you move out and rent it out (unless you retain a right to live there).

Example

Marissa moves from Cardiff to work in San Francisco. With the help of a letting agent she finds a tenant for her house in Cardiff. While the house is being rented out it is not her home.

A property is no longer your home if you move out and do not use it again.

Example

Guy works as a consultant engineer on mining projects in various countries in Africa. He decides to sell his UK property because he won't be spending much time in it over the next few years. On 1 May he moves out of the property and puts his belongings into storage. A short while later he hands over the keys to an estate agent. When he returns to the UK he stays with friends or in hotels. The property is not his home from 1 May, the date he put his belongings into storage.

A home can be a building (such as a conventional house or flat) or a vehicle (e.g. a mobile home) or boat.

Example

Annica and Hugo live in a mobile home and spend their time travelling around the UK. They keep their possessions in the mobile home and sleep in it every night. The mobile home is their home.

A home is a property you own, rent or live in for free.

Example

Justin returns to the UK after studying in the United States for several years. He moves into his parents' house. His parents' house is his home.

A holiday property used for occasional short breaks is not a home.

Example

Dinah lives in London and also owns a villa in Portugal which she uses for her annual holiday (roughly four weeks per year) plus some occasional long weekends. The Portugal property is not her home.

She then decides to stay in the villa from October to March each year to avoid the British winters. The property is no longer being used for occasional short breaks, instead it is her home for part of the year.

Third Automatic UK Test

You will be UK resident if you work "sufficient hours" in the UK for a 365-day period without a significant break.

Generally speaking a significant break is a break of 31 days or more, ignoring leave days.

The following additional criteria must also be met:

- At least some of the 365-day period must be in the tax year.

- More than 75% of your work days during the 365 day period must be UK work days. A work day is one where you do more than three hours work.

- There must be at least one UK work day during the tax year.

Example

Paul travels to the UK on 1 July 2016 and starts working the next day. His job ends on 1 July 2017 and he leaves the UK on 6 August 2017, 400 days after he arrived in the UK.

Over the 365-day period to 30 June 2017 Paul calculates that he worked sufficient hours (see below) in the UK and did not take a significant break.

Some of the 365-day period falls into the 2016/17 tax year and some falls into the 2017/18 tax year.

Over the 365-day period which ends on 30 June 2017 Paul works for over three hours on 240 days, 196 (80%) of which are UK work days. Furthermore, at least one of his UK work days is in 2016/17.

Thus Paul is UK resident for 2016/17 under the third automatic UK test.

Paul also has at least one UK work day during the 2017/18 tax year and is therefore UK resident for that year too.

Calculating Sufficient Hours

So how do you know if you have worked "sufficient hours" in the UK to make you UK resident as part of this test?

Generally speaking you have to work on average 35 hours per week, calculated as follows:

Step 1 – Identify your "disregarded days"
A disregarded day is any day in the 365-day period in which you work more than three hours *overseas*.

Step 2 – Calculate your "net UK hours"
This is the total number of hours you worked in the UK in the 365-day period for all your jobs/trades. Do not include hours worked in the UK on disregarded days.

Step 3 – Calculate your "reference period"
Subtract the following from 365 days:
- Your disregarded days
- Gaps between jobs (up to 15 days for each gap with an overall maximum of 30 per tax year)
- Sick leave
- Annual leave and maternity or paternity leave, providing reasonable in the country in which you are working
- Non-working days embedded within your leave (e.g. weekends and public holidays). Only include non-working days if they are preceded or followed by at least three days of leave

Step 4
Divide the number of days in your reference period by 7. Round down to the nearest whole number. If the answer is less than one, round it up to one.

Step 5
Divide your net UK hours by the number obtained in Step 4.

If the answer is 35 hours or more, you have worked sufficient UK hours for the purposes of the third automatic UK test.

Paperwork

Although the calculation is fairly straightforward if you have all the information at your fingertips, for those who don't keep timesheets etc it could be an absolute nightmare.

Your hours worked have to be calculated over all periods of 365 days, where any part of the 365-day period falls into the tax year, even only one day.

This means you may have to continually calculate your hours until the test is satisfied. It can then be ignored for the rest of the tax year but you will have to start the whole process again at the start of the next tax year.

It's also important to remember the 75% rule. Even if you've worked sufficient UK hours, 75% of your work days during the 365-day period may not have been UK work days. In this case you'll have to see if there is another 365 day period when you do meet the 75% test. If not, then you will not be UK resident under this test.

Summary

You will be UK resident for a particular tax year if:

- *None* of the automatic overseas tests apply to you, and
- Any of the automatic UK tests applies to you

Chapter 6

The Sufficient Ties Test

If you don't meet any of the automatic overseas tests or any of the automatic UK tests you use the sufficient ties test to determine your residence status for the tax year.

This test takes into account your UK ties and the number of days you spend in the UK during the tax year. The more ties you have, the more likely it is that you will be UK resident for tax purposes.

The following ties are considered for this test:

- **Family tie** – your spouse (unless separated) or partner (if you are living together as husband and wife) or children under 18 (with some exceptions) are UK resident.

- **Accommodation tie** – you have a place to live in the UK that is available for a continuous period of 91 days or more during the tax year. You don't have to own the property but must spend at least one night there during the tax year or, if it is the home of a close relative, you must spend at least 16 nights in it in order to have an accommodation tie.

- **Work tie** – you do more than three hours work a day in the UK for a total of at least 40 days. Includes employment and self-employment.

- **90-day tie** – you have spent more than 90 days in the UK in either or both of the previous two tax years.

- **Country tie** – the UK is the country in which you were present for the greatest number of days during the tax year. This tie only applies if you were UK resident in one or more of the previous three tax years.

Ties are then combined with days spent in the UK to determine your residence status. The scoring is different for people who have recently left the UK (i.e. were UK resident in one or more of the previous three tax years) and those who have recently arrived (i.e. were not resident in any of the previous three tax years).

UK Resident in Any of Previous 3 Tax Years – Leavers

UK ties will be combined with days spent in the UK as follows:

Days in UK	Residence status
Fewer than 16 days	Always non-resident
16 – 45 days	UK Resident if 4 or more ties
46 – 90 days	UK Resident if 3 or more ties
91 – 120 days	UK Resident if 2 or more ties
121-182 days	UK Resident if 1 or more ties
183 days or more	Always UK resident

Not Resident in All 3 Previous Tax Years – Arrivers

UK ties will be combined with days spent in the UK as follows:

Days in UK	Resident Status
Fewer than 16 days	Always non-resident
16 – 45 days	Always non-resident
46 – 90 days	UK resident if all 4 ties
91 – 120 days	UK resident if 3 or more ties
121-182 days	UK resident if 2 or more ties
183 days or more	Always UK resident

The Family Tie

You will have a family tie for the tax year if any of the following people are UK resident:

- Your spouse or civil partner (unless you are separated)
- Your partner, if you are "living together as husband and wife"
- Your child if under 18

You can still meet this test even if your partner is living overseas but happens to be UK resident themselves.

The phrase "living together as husband and wife" is not defined in legislation but factors HMRC takes into account are set out here:

www.hmrc.gov.uk/manuals/tctmanual/TCTM09330.htm

You can only have a family tie if your spouse/partner etc is UK resident. If they also have to use the sufficient ties test to work out their own residence status, their family tie with you is ignored.

Example

David and his wife Liz both spend 140 days in the UK. Neither of them was resident in any of the three previous tax years. Under the sufficient ties test they will be UK resident if they have two or more UK ties.

We will assume that both David and Liz have an accommodation tie (see below). If they have a family tie they will both be regarded as UK resident. However, in this case, because the family tie only exists because of their relationship, the tie can be ignored.

As each of them now only has one UK tie neither of them is UK resident.

Children Under 18

If your children under 18 are UK resident this will *not* give you a family tie if you spend time with them in the UK on fewer than 61 days during the tax year.

You will also not have a family tie if your children are only UK resident because they are in full-time education in the UK (at a school, university or college). They must, however, spend fewer than 21 days in the UK outside term time.

Days spent with children outside the UK do not count, so some individuals may wish to fly their children out of the country to avoid acquiring a family tie.

Accommodation Tie

You don't have to own a property in the UK in order to have an accommodation tie. You don't even have to rent a property or have any legal right to use a property.

All that is required is a place to live that is available for several months at a time. So if you can stay with friends or family (or in a hotel) you could end up with an accommodation tie.

More precisely, you will have a UK accommodation tie for the tax year if you have a place to live that is available for a continuous period of 91 days or more during the tax year.

If there is a gap in availability of fewer than 16 days, the gap is ignored and the accommodation is treated as available throughout.

To have an accommodation tie you must also spend at least one night in the accommodation during the tax year.

Example

Justin owns a house in Bristol. He decides to spend a year travelling abroad and rents out his house to fund the trip. Justin therefore has no home in the UK.

His best friend Catriona offers to let him stay in her Bristol flat whenever he's in town. She is happy to let him stay for several months at a time (i.e. her flat is available to him for a continuous period of 91 days or more). Justin stays at the flat for three weeks during the tax year. Justin has an accommodation tie for the tax year.

If Catriona had simply made a casual offer to Justin to stay at her flat "any time" this would not necessarily result in an accommodation tie – she must be prepared to let Justin stay for up to 91 days at a time, even if he doesn't actually stay this long.

Staying With Relatives

If the accommodation is the "home" of a close relative, you can stay there longer – you will only have an accommodation tie if you spend at least 16 nights there during the tax year. Close relatives are your parents, grandparents, brothers and sisters, and children or grandchildren aged 18 or over.

You can avoid acquiring an accommodation tie by staying with close relatives for fewer than 16 nights per tax year. Note, however, that your spouse or partner is *not* considered a close relative. So you may end up with an accommodation tie if you stay with them for just one night during the tax year.

Accommodation versus Home

The terms "accommodation" and "home" are both used in different parts of the Statutory Residence Test but the definitions are completely different.

Remember in Chapter 5 we showed that you can become automatically UK resident if you have a home in the UK.

According to HMRC the main difference between a home and accommodation is that:

"Accommodation can be transient and does not require the degree of stability or permanence that a home does. If an individual does not have a home in the UK they may still have an accommodation tie if they have a place to live in the UK."

A holiday home would not normally count as a "home" under the Statutory Residence Test but could count as available accommodation.

If you stay with relatives you will only end up with an accommodation tie if you stay in their home for 16 nights or more during the tax year.

This is to allow people to stay with family over Christmas without falling foul of the Statutory Residence Test.

Note the use of the word "home". If you stay in a relative's property that is not their home (e.g. their holiday house) you could end up with an accommodation tie if you stay there for just one night.

Accommodation You Own

If you own a property in the UK but rent it out on a commercial basis you will not have an accommodation tie – unless you retain the right to use the property for a period of 91 days or more.

If you own a property in the UK (e.g. a holiday home) but do not spend a night there during the tax year, you will not have an accommodation tie.

Hotels

Short stays at hotels and guesthouses will not usually give you an accommodation tie. However, according to HMRC, if an individual books a room in the same hotel or guesthouse for at least 91 days continuously in a tax year it will be an accommodation tie.

The question is whether short, regular visits to the same hotel could give you an accommodation tie – remember gaps in availability that last fewer than 16 days are ignored.

The simplest way to make sure you do not acquire an accommodation tie is to stay in several hotels.

Comment

This is a very wide test and extremely subjective. Who's to say whether accommodation is "available" for you to use. The taxman could simply argue that any property you stay in is available at any time for as long as you want.

Work Tie

You will have a UK work tie for the tax year if you do more than three hours work a day in the UK on at least 40 days. The days can be intermittent or continuous.

Work takes its every day meaning. If you are an employee, work includes carrying out your duties. If you are self-employed work means time spent carry out your trade, profession or vocation. Voluntary work does not count.

When adding up time spent working you should include:

- Travel time if the cost would have been tax deductible if incurred by you, regardless of whether or not you worked during the journey
- Travel time spent working, regardless of whether the cost would have been tax deductible
- Training paid for by your employer or tax deductible if self-employed
- Time spent serving notice away from work

Transport Workers

There are special rules for international transport workers. If you make a cross-border trip that's starts *in* the UK you will be treated as having worked more than three hours in the UK on that day (even if you spend fewer than three hours working in the UK).

If your cross-border trip starts *outside* the UK, you will be treated as not having worked more than three hours in the UK (unless you make another trip on the same day which starts in the UK).

90-Day Tie

You will have a 90-day tie if you have spent more than 90 days in the UK in either or both of the previous two tax years.

Most recent emigrants will automatically have this tie because most will have spent more than 90 days in the UK in one of the previous two tax years.

Most will also be "leavers" (UK resident in one or more of the previous three tax years).

This means the maximum amount of time they will be able to spend in the UK, while remaining non-resident, is 120 days... but possibly less if they have any other UK ties.

Country Tie

You will have a country tie for the tax year if the UK is the country in which you were present at midnight for the greatest number of days during that tax year.

If it's the same number for two or more countries (one of which is the UK) then you will have a UK tie.

This tie only applies if you were UK resident in one or more of the previous three tax years – i.e. it only applies to "leavers".

Using the Sufficient Ties Test

Many individuals will probably prefer not to rely on the sufficient ties test and will instead limit the number of days they spend in the UK in order to use the automatic overseas tests.

If you do think you will end up using the sufficient ties test it is probably advisable to be conservative. For example you may wish to ensure that you have one less tie than required.

Chapter 7

Leaving the UK: Split Year Treatment

Under the Statutory Residence Test you are either UK resident or non-UK resident for a *whole* tax year.

However, if during the year you start living or working overseas, or come to the UK to live or work, the tax year may be split into two parts:

- a UK part
- an overseas part

This is known as *split-year treatment.*

Split-year treatment does not apply to everyone – you have to qualify. Furthermore, split-year treatment is not optional – if you qualify it is compulsory.

Tax Implications

Splitting the year has important tax implications. You will be taxed as a UK resident for the UK part and you will be taxed as a non-UK resident for the overseas part. Split-year treatment applies to both income tax and capital gains tax.

Broadly speaking, UK tax will not be paid on foreign income or capital gains earned during the overseas part of the year.

Under the Statutory Residence Test it is possible to split a tax year for capital gains tax purposes. In other words, you may be able to sell certain assets in the overseas part of the year and avoid UK capital gains tax.

Split year treatment is not relevant when it comes to deciding if you are UK resident for the purposes of a double taxation agreement. This means that a double tax agreement will override the split-year rules.

When Does Split Year Treatment Apply?

Split-year treatment does NOT apply to everyone who arrives or leaves part way through the tax year. For starters, split-year treatment will only apply if you are actually *UK resident* for the tax year under the Statutory Residence Test.

Example
Pippa comes to the UK to work, having lived in Australia all her life. In the tax year she arrives she spends fewer than 46 days in the country. Under the second automatic overseas test she will be non-resident for the tax year. Split-year treatment will NOT apply to Pippa.

Example
Natasha leaves the UK to live abroad. In the tax year of departure she is UK resident under the Statutory Residence Test. Split-year treatment MAY apply to Natasha.

For split-year treatment to apply, an individual leaving the UK must also be UK resident in the *previous tax year* and non-resident in the *following tax year*. Rather bizarrely, this means that you may not know for certain whether split-year treatment applies to, say, the 2016/17 tax year until the end of the 2017/18 tax year. By then you will have already submitted your tax return for 2016/17!

For split-year treatment to apply to an individual coming to the UK, they must be non-UK resident in the year before the split year.

There are eight situations where the tax year will be split. Cases 1-3 cover people going overseas part way through the tax year, Cases 4-8 cover people coming to the UK part way through the tax year:

- **Case 1** Starting full-time work overseas.
- **Case 2** Partner of someone starting full-time work overseas
- **Case 3** Ceasing to have a home in the UK
- **Case 4** Starting to have a home in the UK only
- **Case 5** Starting full-time work in the UK
- **Case 6** Ceasing full-time work overseas
- **Case 7** Partner of someone ceasing full-time work overseas
- **Case 8** Starting to have a home in the UK

These cases determine *if* split-year treatment will apply and *when* the overseas part of the years starts.

Case 1: Starting Full-time Work Overseas

To qualify for split-year treatment you must be:

- UK resident for the tax year in question
- UK resident for the previous tax year
- Non-UK resident during the next tax year because you meet the third automatic overseas test (see Chapter 4), and
- Satisfy the "overseas work criteria" during the "relevant period"

The first three points are straightforward. The fourth needs a bit more explanation:

Relevant Period

The relevant period starts on the first day you do more than three hours work overseas, it ends on the last day of the tax year. The relevant period is essentially the overseas part of the tax year, when you will be taxed as non-UK resident.

Overseas Work Criteria

You satisfy the overseas work criteria if you:

- Work sufficient hours overseas during the relevant period
- Have no significant break from overseas work during that period. Generally speaking a significant break occurs if 31 days go by and you have not worked for more than three hours on any of those days
- Do not work for more than three hours in the UK on more than the *permitted limit of days* during that period
- Spend no more than the *permitted limit of days* in the UK during that period

How do you know if you've worked sufficient hours overseas during the relevant period? You perform the sufficient hours calculation we examined in Chapter 4 to the relevant period. The one modification is that the maximum number of days you can subtract for gaps between jobs is reduced from 30 days to the permitted limit of days in Table 1.

Table 1
Permitted Limit of Days
Case 1 Starting Full-time Work Overseas

Overseas part of year starts on	Permitted limit UK work days *	Permitted limit Days in UK
6 April to 30 April	30	90
1 May to 31 May	27	82
1 June to 30 June	25	75
1 July to 31 July	22	67
1 Aug to 31 Aug	20	60
1 Sept to 30 Sept	17	52
1 Oct to 31 Oct	15	45
1 Nov to 30 Nov	12	37
1 Dec to 31 Dec	10	30
1 Jan to 31 Jan	7	22
1 Feb to 29 Feb	5	15
1 Mar to 31 Mar	2	7
1 Apr to 5 Apr	0	0

* Also maximum number of days that can be subtracted for gaps between jobs

For example, if your overseas job starts on 20 October you can work for 15 days in the UK until the tax year ends on 5 April. You can spend 45 days in the UK altogether. The closer you are to the end of the tax year, the less time you can spend in the country if you want to enjoy split-year treatment.

Example

Seema has been living in the UK since she was born and is UK resident for tax purposes. She gets a job as a teacher on a three-year contract based in India. She moves there on 10 November 2016 and lives in an apartment provided by her new employer. She meets the overseas work criteria from 10 November 2016.

She returns to the UK to visit her family over the Christmas period for two weeks, and does not work while she is there.

Seema remains working in India throughout the next 2017/18 tax year, only returning for a two-week period over Christmas. Seema will receive split year treatment for the 2016/17 tax year because:

- *She was UK resident for 2015/16 and 2016/17*
- *She is non-UK resident for 2017/18 and meets the third automatic overseas test for that year*

From 10 November 2016 until 5 April 2017 she:

- *Does not work at all in the UK*
- *Spends 14 days in the UK, which is less than the permitted limit of 37 days (see Table 1 above).*

For Seema, the UK part of the tax year will end on 9 November 2016, and the overseas part of the tax year will start on 10 November 2016.

Case 2: The Partner of Someone Starting Full-time Work Overseas

This allows you to enjoy split-year treatment when your partner works overseas. You can either leave during the same tax year or the next one. To qualify for split-year treatment for the current tax year you must:

- Be UK resident for the current tax year
- Be UK resident for the previous tax year
- Be non-UK resident for the next tax year
- Have a partner who qualifies for Case 1 treatment for the current or previous tax year
- Live together in the UK at some point during the current or previous tax year
- Move overseas so that you can live with your partner who is working overseas
- From your "deemed departure day" until the end of the tax year you:

  - Have no home in the UK or, if you have homes both in the UK and overseas, you must spend most of your time in the overseas home
  - Spend no more than the permitted limit of days in the UK

Your partner is your spouse or civil partner. If you're unmarried it's the person with whom you live together as husband and wife.

Your departure day is the later of:

- The day you join your spouse/partner overseas
- Your partner's first overseas day under Case 1

The concept of home is defined in Chapter 5. Remember you don't necessarily have to sell your UK house. You could, for example, rent it out to satisfy this condition.

If you qualify for Case 2 treatment the overseas part of the year (in which you will be taxed as non-UK resident) begins with your departure day and ends on the last day of the tax year.

Example

Clive gets a job overseas and leaves on 1 November 2016. We will assume that he satisfies Case 1 so the 2016/17 tax year is a split year for him.

His partner Jules decides to move abroad and live with him on 1 June 2017 (i.e. during the next 2017/18 tax year).

If Jules satisfies the conditions for Case 2, the 2017/18 tax year will be treated as a split year. If she had moved overseas during the 2016/17 tax year then that tax year would have been a split year for her.

Note that if Clive and Jules return to the UK in 2018/19 and are both UK resident for that tax year, Jules will not qualify for split-year treatment, although Clive will. Remember to qualify for split-year treatment you have to be non-UK resident during the next tax year.

Case 3: Ceasing to Have a Home in the UK

This allows you to enjoy split-year treatment if you go overseas for any other reason than to work. You can enjoy split-year treatment if you leave the UK to live abroad and you no longer have a home in the UK.

To qualify for the current tax year you must be:

- UK resident for the current tax year (e.g. 2017/18)
- UK resident for the previous tax year (e.g. 2016/17)
- Non-resident for the next tax year (e.g. 2018/19), and
- Have one or more UK homes at the start of the tax year and then cease to have any UK homes at some point until the end of the tax year

From the point you no longer have a UK home you must spend fewer than 16 days in the UK until the tax year ends.

From the date you cease to have a UK home you must also show that you have a "sufficient link" with the overseas country by doing *one* of the following:

- Becoming a tax resident in accordance with the country's domestic laws within 6 months, or

- Being present in the overseas country at the end of every day for 6 months, or

- Making sure within 6 months that your only home is in the overseas country (if you have more than one home they must all be in that country).

Some of these conditions are extremely demanding. The requirement to be present in the overseas country at the end of every day for six months means you cannot travel to any other country (not just the UK), unless it's just a day trip.

Alternatively, you cannot have another home in any country other than the overseas country where you are establishing links.

What these conditions mean is that you may not be able to enjoy split-year treatment if you leave the UK to go travelling. You have to establish a link with a single country within six months. Otherwise you will be taxed as UK resident for the whole tax year.

If you do qualify for Case 3 treatment the overseas part of the tax year (in which you will be taxed as non-UK resident) begins on the date you cease to have a home in the UK and ends on the last day of the tax year.

Example

Debbie has been UK resident all her life. While on holiday in New Zealand she meets Jonah, a New Zealand resident. After a whirlwind romance the couple agree to marry and live together in Jonah's home near Auckland.

Debbie puts her UK house on the market and moves out on 10 October 2017, catching a flight to New Zealand a couple of days later. She does not get a job and does not return to the UK for the rest of the tax year.

Debbie does not meet the Case 1 conditions (she doesn't work overseas). She also doesn't meet the Case 2 conditions (she is not accompanying a UK resident working overseas). She does meet the Case 3 conditions:

- *She is UK resident for the current 2017/18 tax year*
- *She is UK resident for the previous 2016/17 tax year*
- *She is non-UK resident in 2018/19*
- *From 10 October 2017 until 5 April 2018 she has no home in the UK and spends fewer than 16 days in the country*
- *She has established her only home is in New Zealand within six months*

Debbie will receive split-year treatment for 2017/18. The overseas part of the tax year starts on 10 October 2017 – the day she no longer has a home in the UK.

When More than One Case Applies

If two or more of Cases 1 to 3 apply then:

- Case 1 has priority over Case 2 and 3
- Case 2 has priority over Case 3

Example

Guy left the UK to start working in South Africa on 1 October 2017. He ceases to have a UK home on 10 February 2018.

Case 1 and Case 3 apply to Guy for the 2017/18 tax year. Case 1 takes priority so the overseas part of the year starts on 1 October 2017.

Chapter 8

Coming to the UK:
Split Year Treatment

Case 4: Starting to Have a Home in the UK Only

You may receive split-year treatment if you come to live in the UK and your only home is in the UK.

To be eligible you must meet the following conditions:

Residence

You must be UK resident for the current tax year – the tax year under consideration.

You must be non-resident for the *previous* tax year.

The Only Home test

You meet the only home test if you have only one home and that home is in the UK. If you have more than one home, all those homes must be in the UK.

For Case 4 split-year treatment, at the start of the tax year you must not meet the only home test. So on 6 April you must NOT have a UK home or, if you do have a UK home, you must also have an overseas home.

At some point during the tax year you must have a UK home and that home must be your only home.

If you do not have a UK home (e.g. you live temporarily with friends or family or in hotels), Case 4 will not be satisfied and you may be taxed as UK resident for the entire tax year.

The Sufficient Ties Test

To be eligible for split-year treatment it is also essential that you do not have any UK ties or insufficient ties to meet the sufficient ties test. The sufficient ties test is covered in Chapter 6.

More precisely, you must not have sufficient UK ties for the period 6 April to the day before you meet the only home test.

Overseas Part of the Tax Year

The overseas part of the tax year starts on 6 April (the beginning of the tax year) and ends the day before you meet the only home in the UK test. The UK part of the tax year runs from that point until the end of the tax year

Example

Rory has been living in Australia for the last five years. He has no UK ties. He decides to return to the UK and sells his house in Perth and moves out in June 2017. On 1 July 2017 he arrives back in the UK and on 15 July he signs a 12 month lease on a Newcastle flat. On 1 August he starts a new job.

Rory is eligible for split-year treatment under Case 4 in 2017/18 because:

- *He was non-resident in the previous tax year (2016/17)*
- *He is UK resident for current tax year (2017/18)*
- *He started to have his only home in the UK during the current tax year and this state of affairs continued until the end of the tax year*
- *He had no UK ties from 6 April 2017 to 15 July 2017 (the date he started to have his only home in the UK)*

The overseas part of the tax year starts on 6 April and ends on 14 July 2017. The UK part of the tax year starts on 15 July, the day he started to have his only home in the UK.

Rory may also be eligible for split-year treatment under Case 5 (starting full-time work in the UK). Priority is given to the case with the shortest overseas part so Case 4 has priority over Case 5. If Case 4 cannot be satisfied, Case 8 may apply (the requirements are similar except you are not prohibited from having an overseas home.)

Case 5: Starting Full-time Work in the UK

You may receive split-year treatment for a tax year if you start to work full-time in the UK.

Case 6: Ceasing Full-time Work Overseas

In some circumstances you may receive split-year treatment if you were non-UK resident in the previous tax year because you worked full-time overseas and you cease working during the tax year.

Case 7: Partner of Someone Ceasing Full-time Work Overseas

If you have been living abroad with someone in full-time employment overseas and they stop working overseas and return to the UK and you decide to join them, you may qualify for split-year treatment.

Case 8: Starting to Have a Home in the UK

If you have no home in the UK but at some point during the tax year you start to have a home in the UK then you may qualify for split-year treatment.

For more information about these cases go to:

www.hmrc.gov.uk/international/rdr3.pdf

Chapter 9

Temporary Non-Residence: New Anti-Avoidance Rules

If you return to the UK after a period of *temporary non-residence*, you may have to pay tax on certain income and capital gains realized during that period of temporary non-residence.

The anti-avoidance provisions only kick in if you are non-resident for five years or less.

If you don't want these rules to apply, your period of non-residence must last for more than five years, for example from 4 November 2017 to 11 November 2022.

Note, your period of non-residence does not necessarily start when you leave the UK – it could start *before* you leave or *after* you leave. In other words, you may have to live overseas for more than five years or less than five years in order to shelter your income and capital gains from UK tax.

It is therefore critically important to determine when your period of non-residence starts and ends.

Departures before 2013/14

The new rules only apply to 2013/14 and later tax years. If the year of your departure was 2012/13 or earlier, the old rules still apply.

Short-term Visitors

The anti-avoidance provisions do not apply to people who have only lived in the UK for a few years – generally speaking, they only apply if you were UK resident for four or more of the previous seven tax years.

Using slightly more precise language, you can only be regarded as temporarily non-resident if, in four or more of the seven tax years immediately before your year of departure, you had either:

- Sole UK residence
- Sole UK residence for the UK part of any split year

An individual's residence status for tax years before 2013/14 (i.e. before the Statutory Residence Test came into being) is determined using the old residence rules and not the Statutory Residence Test.

What Income is Affected?

The anti-avoidance provisions do not apply to all types of income – they generally only affect income that you can manipulate, i.e. income that you can halt while UK resident and pay yourself in a large lump sum while non-resident. This includes:

- Capital gains
- Withdrawals from flexible drawdown pension funds
- Dividends from limited companies
- Directors loans that are written off

Normal salary, self-employment profits, bank interest and dividends from stock market companies and most regular pension income is not affected.

Temporary Non-Residence – Starting Date

Your period of temporary non-residence starts when you are no longer *solely UK resident.*

You will be solely UK resident if you are UK resident and at no time treaty non-resident. You are treaty non-resident if you are regarded as resident elsewhere under a double taxation agreement.

Your temporary non-residence may start at the beginning of a tax year or part way through a tax year in the case of split years.

What you have to determine is the last residence period (whole tax year or UK part of a split year) in which you are solely UK resident. That marks the end of your UK residence and the start of your period of non-residence. The period of non-residence ends on the day before you have sole UK residence again.

Example 1

Natasha has lived in the UK all her life. On 10 October 2017 she moves to El Salvatore. We'll assume she does not qualify for split-year treatment. Thus the residence period we're looking for is the final full tax year when she is solely UK resident.

Under the Statutory Residence Test Natasha is UK resident for the 2017/18 tax year – she doesn't meet any of the automatic overseas tests and she has lived in the UK for 187 days during the tax year and is therefore UK resident under the first automatic UK test.

We will also assume that under the Statutory Residence Test Natasha is non-UK resident for the whole of the 2018/19 tax year under the third automatic overseas test.

Natasha's period of non-residence therefore starts on 6 April 2018 – almost six months after leaving the UK.

In this example we have also assumed that El Salvatore does not have a double tax treaty with the UK. Such a tax treaty could make Natasha non-resident from an earlier date.

Example 2

Ross has lived in the UK all his life. On 1 June 2017 he leaves the UK to work abroad. He returns to the UK on 1 August 2022.

He qualifies for Case 1 split-year treatment. When he returns he qualifies for Case 4 split-year treatment.

Ross has sole UK residence for the residence period 6 April 2017 to 31 May 2017 (assuming he starts work on 1 June).

His period of non-residence therefore starts on 1 June 2017. Ross's period of non-residence ends on 31 July 2022 and he is solely UK resident from 1 August 2022 until 5 April 2023.

His period of temporary non-residence runs from 1 June 2017 to 31 July 2022 – just over five years. Thus Ross is not subject to the temporary non-residence provisions.

Example 3

James has lived in the UK all his life. On 15 March 2018 (i.e. during the 2017/18 tax year) he moves to Europia and is considered resident there from that point onwards. In terms of the Statutory Residence Test he is also UK resident up to the end of the tax year on 5 April 2018. From 15 March to 5 April James is considered treaty non-resident.

James does not qualify for split-year treatment, so the period of temporary non-residence will start at the beginning of a tax year.

Although James was UK resident in 2017/18 he was not solely UK resident (he was also resident in Europia). James was solely UK resident in 2016/17. So his period of non-residence starts at the beginning of the 2017/18 tax year on 6 April 2017 – even though he left the UK on 15 March 2018.

James returns to the UK on 18 June 2021 and split-year treatment applies. James has sole UK residence from 18 June 2021. He is treaty resident for the UK part of the year. His temporary non-residence ends on 17 June 2021.

The period of temporary non-residence is 6 April 2017 to 17 June 2021 inclusive which is less than five years so James is subject to the temporary non-residence provisions.

Example 4

Emma has lived in the UK all her life but leaves on 1 July 2018 to work in Tangola. She qualifies for split-year treatment for the 2018/19 tax year.

Tangola's tax year runs from January to December and under domestic tax law Emma is treated as resident in Tangola for the whole of 2018.

Tangola and the UK have a double tax treaty and using the tie-breaker tests, Emma is resident in Tangola for the whole of 2018.

So although 2018/19 is a split year, the period from 6 April 2018 to 31 June 2018 is not a period of sole UK residence – she is treaty non-resident during that time.

Emma is also treaty non-resident from 1 January 2018 to 5 April 2018. This is part of the 2017/18 tax year, so she does not have sole UK residence during 2017/18 either.

As a result her period of sole UK residence ends on 5 April 2017 and her period of temporary non-residence starts on 6 April 2017, almost 15 months before she leaves the UK.

Let's say Emma returns to the UK on 16 October 2022. In terms of the UK/Tangola double tax treaty she is Tangolan resident for the whole of 2022. Thus although split year treatment applies she is not solely UK resident for the UK part of the split year (16 October 2022 to 5 April 2023).

We therefore have to look to the next full tax year which starts on 6 April 2023. This is the first residence period in which she is solely UK resident.

Overall Emma's period of non-residence runs for six years from 6 April 2017 to 5 April 2023, even though she is only out of the country for less than four and a half years.

In this example Emma clearly benefits form the fact that Tangola's tax year runs from January to December and she is treaty non-resident for the whole of 2018.

Chapter 10

Temporary Non-Residence: Capital Gains Tax

Under the old rules, to avoid capital gains tax on assets sold while non-UK resident, you had to remain non-resident for at least five complete tax years.

So if you left the UK in May the five-year countdown would only start almost a year later on 6 April.

The old rules still apply to departures that took place before the 2013/14 tax year.

Under the current anti-avoidance rules, to avoid capital gains tax you have to be non-resident for **more than five years** (tax years are not relevant).

If you are non-resident for less than five years your capital gains will be taxed when you return to the UK. Relief is available for any foreign tax paid.

As we saw in Chapter 9, the actual amount of time you have to live outside the UK could be less than five years, for example if you are treaty non-resident.

The anti-avoidance rules generally do not apply to assets acquired and sold during your period of temporary non-residence. So if you buy an asset while you are non-resident and sell it while you are non-resident, you will generally not be subject to UK capital gains tax, even if you have been non-resident for less than five years.

There are, however, some restrictions to prevent this rule being abused. For example, if a husband transfers an asset to his wife that he acquired while UK resident, she may become subject to capital gains tax if she returns to the UK within five years, even though she may have "acquired" and sold the asset while non-resident.

Residential Property Gains

Even if you are non-resident for more than five years, you may still be subject to tax on some of your gains from UK *residential* property.

Since 6 April 2015, a new capital gains tax charge has been levied on non-residents disposing of UK residential property.

Other types of property (e.g. commercial property) and other types of assets are not affected.

Furthermore, the new charge only applies to that part of the gain that arose *after* 5 April 2015.

We'll take a closer look at these rules in Part 3 but what they mean is you can no longer use emigration as a way to completely escape UK capital gains tax on your residential properties.

However, because the charge only applies to post 5 April 2015 gains, you may be able to use a period of temporary non-residence to avoid paying tax on most of your capital gains.

Chapter 11

Temporary Non-Residence: Dividends

It used to be possible to become non-resident for a very short period of time and extract tax-free dividends from a company. The anti-avoidance rules now clamp down on this practice if the dividends are paid during a period of temporary non-residence.

In the year you return the dividends will be added to your other income and taxed. A credit will be allowed for any overseas tax paid on the income.

Post Departure Profits

The anti-avoidance rule does not apply to "post-departure trade profits". If your company makes profits while you are non-resident, dividends that are paid out of these profits will not be taxed when you return to the UK.

Post-departure trade profits are trade profits that arise in an accounting period (financial year) that begins after your period of temporary non-residence has started.

If the accounting period straddles the start of your period of temporary non-residence, you have to calculate how much of the profit can be attributed to the period of non-residence.

What Dividends Are Affected?

The anti-avoidance rules apply if the dividends are received from

- A close company (or similar overseas company), and
- You are a material participator in the company (or an "associate" of yours is a material participator)

A close company is a company that has five or fewer shareholders or any number of shareholders if those shareholders are directors.

The vast majority of small owner-managed companies are close companies.

A material participator is someone who controls more than 5% of the ordinary shares in the company or is entitled to receive more than 5% of the assets if the company is wound up.

Associates include your close relatives (including your spouse, parents, grandparents, children, grandchildren and brothers and sisters).

Loans Written Off

Many company owners borrow money from their companies. For example, if the company doesn't have any profits it cannot pay dividends. A higher salary is one solution in these circumstances but this often results in a hefty national insurance bill (there is no national insurance on dividends).

As an alternative, the company owner can take a loan from the company and repay it when the company has enough profit to declare dividends.

Sometimes the company may formally write off the loan. The amount waived is then taxed as a deemed dividend. Where the shareholder is a director or employee the amount written off is also treated as earnings and subject to class 1 national insurance.

If the loan is written off during a period of temporary non-residence it will treated as having been written off in the year you return.

Tax Planning Pointers

Income tax can still be avoided by remaining non-resident for more than five years, so long-term emigrants will not be affected.

If you fall foul of the anti-avoidance provisions all your dividends will be bunched together and taxed in the tax year you return. You will not be able to access any unused personal allowance or basic-rate band from previous tax years. Thus you could end up paying much more tax than if you had remained UK resident.

Chapter 12

Transitional Rules

The Statutory Residence Test applies from the 2013/14 tax year onwards. However, when applying the test you may need to know your residence status for *previous* tax years, i.e. before the test applied.

To provide greater certainty individuals can elect to use the Statutory Residence Test for previous years to help them determine their residence status for the tax years 2013/14 to 2017/18.

Example

Debbie spent 20 days in the UK during the 2013/14 tax year. Under the automatic overseas tests (see Chapter 4) she was non-resident IF she was also non-resident in all of the previous three tax years (she can spend up to 45 days in the UK). However, if she was UK resident in any of the previous three tax years she will not be able to use the automatic overseas tests (as a leaver she can only spend up to 15 days in the UK).

It all boils down to her residence status in the previous three tax years, i.e. before the Statutory Residence Test came into operation. Debbie works out that, using the Statutory Residence Test, she would have been non-resident in 2010/11, 2011/12 and 2012/13. She therefore elects to use the transitional rules and is treated as non-resident in 2013/14.

Note that this does not affect her actual residence status for the 2010/11, 2011/12 and 2012/13 tax years and HMRC could still challenge her residence status for those tax years. Her actual residence status for those earlier years will still be determined by the old rules as set out in HMRC's booklet HMRC6.

Elections to use the Statutory Residence Test for previous tax years are irrevocable and must be made in writing, either on your tax return or in a letter sent to HMRC.

The election must generally be made within a year of the end of the year to which it applies. For example, for 2013/14 the election had to be made by 5 April 2015. Separate elections are required for later tax years.

Part 2

Non-Residents: Income Tax Planning

Chapter 13

Are You Entitled to a Personal Allowance?

Non-residents have to continue paying income tax on most of their *UK income*. However, most are entitled to an income tax personal allowance.

The personal allowance for 2017/18 is £11,500. This means couples can shelter up to £23,000 of UK income from tax.

Who Qualifies for a Personal Allowance?

The vast majority of non-residents have the right to claim a UK personal allowance. In terms of the legislation the following individuals qualify:

- British citizens
- EEA nationals*
- Residents of the Isle of Man and the Channel Islands
- Persons previously resident in the UK and resident abroad for the sake of their health or that of a family member
- Crown servants
- Employees in the service of any territory under Her Majesty's protection
- Persons employed by a missionary society
- Persons whose late spouse was employed in the service of the Crown

*EEA countries include: Austria, Belgium, Bulgaria, Cyprus, Czech Republic, Denmark, Estonia, Finland, France, Germany, Greece, Hungary, Iceland, Ireland, Italy, Latvia, Liechtenstein, Lithuania, Luxembourg, Malta, Netherlands, Norway, Poland, Portugal, Romania, Slovakia, Slovenia, Spain, Sweden and the United Kingdom.

It used to be possible to claim a personal allowance on the grounds of being a Commonwealth citizen. This is no longer possible.

Double Tax Treaties

Many non-residents also qualify for a personal allowance under the provisions of double tax treaties.

These include:

- Nationals of Israel or Jamaica (passports will provide proof if required)

- An individual who is a **national** and **resident** of: Argentina, Australia, Azerbaijan, Bangladesh, Belarus, Bolivia, Bosnia-Herzegovina, Botswana, Canada, Egypt, Gambia, India, Indonesia, Ivory Coast, Japan, Jordan, Kazakhstan, South Korea, Lesotho, Malaysia, Montenegro, Morocco, New Zealand, Nigeria, Oman, Pakistan, Papua New Guinea, Philippines, Russian Federation, Serbia, South Africa, Sri Lanka, Sudan, Switzerland, Taiwan, Thailand, Trinidad and Tobago, Tunisia, Turkey, Turkmenistan, Uganda, Ukraine, Uzbekistan, Venezuela, Vietnam and Zimbabwe.

  You must get a certificate from the local tax authority stating that you are resident there for tax purposes. You must also have a document (e.g. a passport) to prove that you are a national.

- An individual who is a **resident** of: Austria, Barbados, Belgium, Burma, Fiji, Greece, Ireland, Kenya, Luxembourg, Mauritius, Namibia, Netherlands, Portugal, Swaziland or Switzerland.

  Again you must get a certificate from the local tax authority stating that you are resident there for tax purposes.

If you are a resident but not a national of any of the following countries you are not entitled to a personal allowance if your income consists solely of dividends, interest or royalties: Austria, Belgium, Kenya, Luxembourg, Mauritius, Portugal or Switzerland.

US citizens residing in the USA are not entitled to personal allowances under the UK/USA double tax agreement.

Dealing with HMRC

If you are entitled to a personal allowance you can claim it by completing form R43.

The form can be found by entering "HMRC R43" into a search engine like Google.

This form can also be used to claim a repayment of some or all of the UK tax you have paid in the current or previous tax years. You may be entitled to a refund if, for example:

- You have interest from a UK bank account and 20% tax was deducted (see Chapter 16).

- You have UK rental income and your letting agent or tenants have already paid 20% tax on the income (see Chapter 14).

You do not use this form if you also complete a UK tax return.

Restricting Personal Allowance for Non-Residents

In the 2014 Budget the Government announced that it would consult on restricting the personal allowance for non-residents. In the end it decided not to act but stated that:

"The government will continue to discuss implementation of this change with stakeholders. Should the government decide to proceed, a more detailed consultation will be undertaken."

Chapter 14

How to Pay Less Tax on UK Rental Income

If you are UK resident for tax purposes you have to pay UK income tax on your *worldwide* rental profits.

If you are non-UK resident you do not have to pay UK income tax on foreign rental properties. You do, however, have to pay income tax on rental properties situated in the UK.

Example 1

Ernest owns 20 rental properties, all situated outside the UK. If Ernest is UK resident he will pay UK income tax on his rental profits. If Ernest is non-UK resident he will not pay any UK income tax on his rental profits.

Example 2

Harry, a UK resident, earns all of his income from a portfolio of UK properties. He does not have any other income. If Harry becomes non-UK resident he will continue to pay the same amount of UK income tax. He will not save a penny in tax by becoming non-UK resident.

Example 3

Debbie owns a portfolio of UK and foreign rental properties. Her UK property business produces a rental profit of £20,000 per year. Her foreign property business produces a rental profit of £10,000 per year. If Debbie is UK resident she will pay UK income tax on her worldwide rental profits: £30,000. If Debbie is non-UK resident she will pay UK tax on her £20,000 UK rental profits only.

Although as a non-resident you will continue to pay UK tax on your UK rental profits, it's possible that you will pay much less tax than before. There are also steps you can take to reduce the sting. Before we turn our attention to tax planning, it is important to explain the Non-Resident Landlord Scheme which HMRC uses to collect tax from letting agents and tenants.

The Non-Resident Landlord Scheme

Non-resident landlords have 20% tax deducted from their rental income by their letting agents. The tax is paid to HMRC quarterly.

Where there is no letting agent the tenant must deduct the tax and pay it to HMRC quarterly, although this is not necessary if the rent is £100 per week or less (£5,200 per year). If two or more people are tenants under the lease the £5,200 limit applies separately to each tenant.

When the non-resident landlord completes his tax return the tax deducted by the letting agent or tenant is taken off the final tax bill. Any excess tax can be reclaimed.

Although it is called the *Non-resident* Landlord Scheme it only applies to landlords (including companies) whose "usual place of abode" is outside the UK.

For individuals, HMRC takes absences from the UK that last six months or more as meaning that your usual place of abode is outside the UK. So you could be a UK resident for tax purposes but still fall within the ambit of the scheme.

Non-resident landlords can apply to have their rental income paid gross with no tax deducted if:

- Their tax affairs are up to date, or

- They have never had any UK tax obligations before, or

- They do not expect to be liable to pay UK tax (for example, if their rental income is covered by their personal allowance)

You can apply to receive your rent with no tax deducted by using form NRL1.

You can find this form by typing "HMRC NRL1" into a search engine like Google.

HMRC will then inform your letting agent or tenant in writing that you are approved to receive rental income with no tax deducted.

The fact that you are approved does not mean your rental income is tax free. It is still subject to UK income tax and must be included on your annual tax return if you have to complete one.

Having your rental income paid gross may be attractive if you expect your final tax bill to be less than the tax deducted by your letting agent or tenant (for many landlords this will be the case).

Having your rental income paid gross is also attractive if you do not want to use a letting agent to save on costs and do not think your tenants will cope with the admin burden.

A friend or relative who manages your properties may also have to operate the Non-Resident Landlord Scheme if they handle your rental income.

If you pay someone to find tenants but they do not handle or control any of your rental income they do not have to operate the Non-Resident Landlord Scheme. In these cases it is the tenant who has to deduct the tax and pay it to HMRC.

How Letting Agents & Tenants Calculate Your Tax

Letting agents and tenants withhold 20% tax from your gross rental income but can deduct certain deductible expenses they have paid, for example payments for property repairs and letting agent fees.

The letting agent or tenant must provide you with an annual certificate that details the total amount of tax paid for the year on your behalf:

You can find this form by typing "HMRC NRL6" into a search engine like Google.

When you complete your tax return you can then set off the tax on this certificate against your overall tax bill.

20% Tax versus Actual Tax

The 20% tax deducted by your letting agent or tenant could be different to your final tax bill for several reasons:

- You may be entitled to a personal allowance which could shelter thousands of pounds of your rental profits from tax (£11,500 in 2017/18).

- You may have additional property expenses that can be deducted from the income. Letting agents cannot deduct expenses paid by the landlord.

- You may be subject to higher-rate tax at 40% or additional rate tax at 45% if you have a lot of rental income.

Why Non-Residents May Pay Less Tax

Although your UK rental profits will remain taxable when you become non-resident, it is possible that you will pay less tax than before.

Example

Serge is UK resident and earns a salary of £50,000 plus rental profits of £15,000. As a higher-rate taxpayer Serge pays 40% tax on his rental profits: £6,000.

He then gets a job overseas and becomes non-UK resident. His overseas salary is not subject to UK tax. His rental profits are his only UK income now. In 2017/18 the first £11,500 is tax free, being covered by his income tax personal allowance. The remaining £3,500 is taxed at 20%: £700.

The tax on his rental income has fallen from £6,000 to £700. His effective tax rate is just 5%.

Before Serge became non-resident his personal allowance and basic-rate band were used up by his salary income. Now that he is non-resident these can be used against his rental income.

Renting Out Your Home

You may go abroad to work or for some other reason but plan to return to the UK at some point in the future. If you do this you may decide to keep your UK home and rent it out while you are living overseas.

The rental profit will be taxable but it is possible that some or all of this income will end up being tax free thanks to your income tax personal allowance.

Example
Paul accepted a job offer in Hong Kong and moved there with his wife Louise. The couple plan to return to the UK eventually and have decided to keep the family home they own together and rent it out for £1,500 per month. They do not have any other UK income.

Paul and Louise are both British citizens and therefore entitled to a UK personal allowance of £11,500 each in 2017/18. The annual rent is £18,000 and fully covered by their personal allowances. There is no UK tax payable.

Although their rental income is £18,000 their taxable rental *profit* will be lower if they have tax deductible expenses. These expenses do not affect the outcome in this example because the couple's rental income is fully covered by their personal allowances.

Splitting Rental Income – Couples

Couples can minimise the income tax payable on their rental income by choosing the optimal ownership split for their buy-to-let properties. The optimal split may change after you become non-resident.

Example
Clive and his wife Julie live in Manchester. Clive earns a salary of £80,000. His wife Julie doesn't have a job but manages the couple's property portfolio and earns rental profits of £40,000 per year. The couple decided to keep all the properties in Julie's name to save income tax. If the rental income was split equally, Clive would pay £8,000 tax on his share (40% x £20,000), whereas Julie currently pays just £4,000 on this income (20% x £20,000). The total tax saving is £4,000.

Example revised

Clive and Julie are non-UK resident for tax purposes. Clive earns a salary of £80,000 which is not taxed in the UK. Julie has rental profits of £40,000 from UK properties. The couple have no other income. In 2017/18 the first £11,500 of Julie's rental profits are tax free, the remaining £28,500 is taxed at 20%. Her total tax bill is £5,700. If Julie's rental profits rise above the higher-rate threshold (£45,000 in 2017/18) she will start paying tax at 40%.

As things stand Clive's UK personal allowance and basic-rate band are being wasted because he has no UK income. If half the properties are owned by Clive the annual income tax bill on the rental income will fall from £5,700 to £3,400 and any future increase in their rental income will be taxed at just 20% and not 40%.

The ownership split of a property can be changed but there may be legal costs and taxes to pay, including capital gains tax (if the couple are not married) and stamp duty land tax (if there is a mortgage over the property). It may also be necessary to obtain permission from the lender.

These issues and potential solutions are covered in the Taxcafe guides *How to Save Property Tax* and *How to Save Tax*.

Mortgage Issues

If you intend to rent out your home in the UK after becoming non-resident you will probably have to obtain your lender's permission. You may be charged a fee for this and any consent may be subject to a time limit. You may also be subject to a higher interest rate or forced to take out a buy-to-let mortgage.

What happens to your rental properties when you emigrate? According to Ray Boulger, senior technical manager at mortgage broker John Charcol, commercial mortgages normally have a condition requiring such a change to be notified to the lender but most buy-to-let mortgages do not.

However, because borrowers are required to notify lenders of their change of address, this may prompt the lender to ask some questions.

Mr Boulger also points out that becoming non-resident could

affect your ability to take out new mortgages or remortgage existing properties because only a small proportion of buy-to-let lenders currently offer their products to expats.

For example, if your existing fixed-rate deals come to an end while you are non-resident, you may be stuck paying the lender's standard variable rate (or other "revert to" rate) unless you can find new fixed-rate deals from another lender who is willing to deal with expats.

The change in your tax status may also affect your ability to borrow. According to Mr Boulger: "Because of the income tax changes starting in April (see below) some lenders now take into account the borrower's marginal rate when assessing affordability and so, depending on the tax situation of the borrower, the affordability calculation may change when becoming an expat. This normally won't impact the existing mortgage but it might affect the maximum loan if the landlord wanted a further advance or to remortgage."

Could your lender impose some sort of penalty or take any other action against you once they discover you are non-resident? According to Boulger it would be extremely unusual for a lender to either ask for a mortgage to be repaid or to take a borrower off their current deal just because the borrower had become an expat.

"Even if they did, and especially if they tried to impose any early repayment charges, the borrower could complain that this contravened the FCA's 'treating customers fairly' rule. Although most buy-to-let mortgages are not regulated by the FCA, lenders who are regulated by it are nevertheless required to comply with its general principles, even for non regulated lending.

"An exception where a lender might understandably be more aggressive could be where someone became an expat very soon after applying for the mortgage, in which case the lender might ask if this was information which was known to the borrower at the time of the application and should have been disclosed."

Needless to say, it is essential to obtain advice about your existing UK mortgages before you leave the country.

Tax Relief on Mortgage Interest

From 6 April 2017 onwards (the start of the 2017/18 tax year) the Government is starting to restrict tax relief on interest and finance costs paid by individual landlords (including non-resident landlords) who own residential properties.

The new rules will not apply to commercial property or furnished holiday lettings or to properties held inside companies.

Higher-rate tax relief for interest and finance costs is being phased out over a four-year period as follows:

2017/18	75% deducted as normal, 25% at basic rate only
2018/19	50% deducted as normal, 50% at basic rate only
2019/20	25% deducted as normal, 75% at basic rate only
2020/21	All relieved at basic rate only from this year on

It's possible that these changes will have less impact or no impact at all on some non-resident landlords.

Example

To keep things simple we'll assume it's the 2020/21 tax year (when the mortgage tax relief restriction will have full force). Dennis is a UK resident with a salary of £60,000. He also has rental income of £40,000 and property expenses of £6,000, so his taxable rental profit is £34,000. He also pays £14,000 in mortgage interest but none of this is deductible when calculating his taxable rental profit.

With this much salary Dennis is a higher-rate taxpayer and will pay 40% tax on the £34,000 taxable rental profit – £13,600. He'll also get a tax reduction equal to 20% of his interest – £2,800. He pays a total of £10,800 tax on his rental income. This is £2,800 more than he would have paid if his interest was fully deductible, as it was in the past.

Example revised

This time we will assume Dennis is non-resident. He still earns a salary of £60,000 but none of this is taxable in the UK. With no other UK income the first £12,500 of his £34,000 taxable rental profit will be tax free (the Government has promised to increase the personal allowance to at least £12,500 by 2020/21). Income tax at 20% will be payable on the remainder – £4,300. He will also enjoy a tax reduction equal to 20% of his mortgage interest – £2,800. In total he pays £1,500 income tax on his rental income.

The important point to note is that Dennis would have paid the exact same amount of tax if his mortgage interest was fully tax deductible, as it was prior to 2017/18. In other words, he is unaffected by the mortgage tax relief restriction.

Even though his mortgage interest is no longer a tax deductible expense, his taxable rental profit is not big enough to push him into the 40% tax bracket. He pays 20% tax on a bigger chunk of his rental income but also receives an identical 20% tax reduction.

Overseas Lenders

If you take out a mortgage for a UK property with an overseas lender, the interest payments may be subject to UK withholding tax if the interest is treated as being paid from a UK source. If withholding tax does apply it may be possible to apply for an exemption if there is a double tax agreement between the UK and the country where the lender is based.

This is a complex area and your lender or mortgage adviser may be able to provide additional guidance.

Overseas Tax Implications

Your rental income may also be taxed in the country you move to. The rules differ from country to country but, generally speaking, the tax you pay in the UK will be allowed as a credit against your overseas tax bill.

It is possible to escape any overseas tax bill by moving to a country where there is no income tax or a country that does not tax foreign income (i.e. UK income). See Chapter 20 for more details.

If you move to a country that *generally* has lower tax rates than the UK you may still have additional overseas tax to pay if your UK tax bill is very small (e.g. if most of your rental income is covered by your personal allowance).

If your rental income IS taxed overseas, any tax planning you do to reduce your UK tax bill (e.g. splitting rental income with your spouse or partner) could be undone in the country you move to. For this reason it is essential to consider both the UK and overseas tax implications of any tax planning you carry out.

Earlier we showed how Clive and Julie were able to reduce their UK tax bill by splitting their rental income when they became non-resident. This allowed them to utilize two personal allowances and two basic-rate bands.

However, if Clive ends up paying a lot of additional overseas tax on his UK rental income (because he also earns a salary overseas and has a high marginal tax rate) it is possible that the couple will end up paying more tax overall. It may be worth keeping all the rental income in Julie's name.

Chapter 15

How to Pay Less Tax on UK Dividends

If you own a UK company, you generally can't take it with you when you become non-resident. The company's profits will usually continue to be subject to UK corporation tax. The corporation tax rate is falling from 20% to 19% in April 2017 and to 17% in April 2020.

The after-tax profits of the company can then be extracted as dividends. Non-residents can avoid UK income tax on dividends because dividends and certain other types of "disregarded income" (e.g. interest income) are subject to special tax rules.

Salaries, rental income and self-employment profits are not disregarded income and are always fully taxed.

Before we examine how the dividend income of non-residents is taxed, it's important to first explain how *UK residents* are taxed.

Dividends – How UK Residents Are Taxed

Dividends are subject to income tax but not national insurance. The income tax rates on dividends are lower than the income tax rates on salaries and other types of income because dividends are paid out of a company's *after-tax profits*, i.e. after the company has paid corporation tax.

The tax treatment of dividends has completely changed with effect from 6 April 2016 (the start of the 2016/17 tax year).

Dividend tax credits have been abolished, so it is no longer necessary to gross up your cash dividends to calculate your tax. All tax calculations now work with cash dividends only and are therefore a lot simpler.

(I generally refer to the amount of dividend actually paid, or deemed to be paid, as the "cash" dividend. This does not necessarily mean that it is literally paid in cash, as dividends are sometimes paid by way of accounting entries.)

While simpler tax calculations are the good news, the bad news is that new tax rates for cash dividends have been introduced that are 7.5% higher than the previous ones.

The first £5,000 of dividend income you receive is currently tax free thanks to the "dividend nil rate band", also known as the "dividend allowance". However, in the March 2017 Budget it was announced that the dividend allowance will be cut to £2,000 in 2018/19.

For those receiving dividends in excess of the dividend allowance, the following income tax rates apply (the old effective rates are included for comparison):

	Old	Current
Basic-rate taxpayers	0%	7.5%
Higher-rate taxpayers	25%	32.5%
Additional-rate taxpayers	30.6%	38.1%

For more detailed information about the tax treatment of dividends and tax planning information for UK resident company owners, see the Taxcafe guide *Salary versus Dividends*.

The recent tax increase clearly makes it more attractive to pay yourself dividends while you are non-resident, if possible.

Dividends – How Non-Residents Are Taxed

Non-residents can avoid paying tax on their UK dividends but there isn't a blanket tax exemption – it's a bit more complicated than that.

Section 811 of the Income Tax Act limits the amount of tax non-residents have to pay by comparing two tax calculations. In the first your tax liability is calculated the normal way. In the second certain types of income, like dividends, are excluded (the good news) but your personal allowance is taken away (the bad news).

If the second tax calculation produces a lower tax bill than that calculation is used.

Disregarded income includes:

- Interest from banks and building societies
- Dividends from UK companies
- Income from unit trusts
- Income from National Savings & Investments products
- Certain social security benefits, e.g. state pensions
- Taxable income from purchased life annuities except annuities under personal pension schemes

According to HMRC, the restriction on the tax payable on investment income is not available for any tax year in which split-year treatment applies (see Chapter 7).

You might also be able to obtain tax relief under the terms of a double tax agreement, if one applies.

In summary, as a non-resident you can receive tax-free dividends from UK companies BUT your personal allowance will be taken away, which means you could pay more tax on any other UK income you have, for example rental income.

Two tax calculations must be performed to see which produces the smallest tax bill:

- One for all your UK income with the personal allowance.

- One for some of your income (i.e. excluding your dividends and other disregarded income) but without the personal allowance.

In terms of Section 399 of the Income Tax (Trading and Other Income) Act, a non-resident who receives a UK dividend is treated as having paid tax on that distribution at the dividend ordinary rate (currently 7.5%).

HMRC has produced very little guidance but it would appear that, when preparing the two calculations, you will receive a non-refundable tax credit of 7.5% in the first calculation that includes the dividend income.

If you don't have any other taxable income apart from your dividend income (e.g. rental income) it doesn't matter if you lose your personal allowance and your dividends will be tax free.

Furthermore, it should also be remembered that UK residents also have their personal allowances withdrawn when their income exceeds £100,000. Once your income exceeds £123,000 in 2017/18 your personal allowance will have disappeared completely.

How Much Tax Can Non-Residents Save?

It's important to remember that basic-rate taxpayers (those with income up to £45,000 in 2017/18) pay at most 7.5% income tax on their dividend income. Dividends that fall within the £11,500 personal allowance or £5,000 dividend allowance are tax free.

For example, a UK resident company owner who receives dividend income of £45,000 in 2017/18 and has no other income will pay no tax on the first £16,500 thanks to their personal allowance and dividend allowance and will pay just £2,138 tax on the remaining £28,500.

(The basic-rate band in 2017/18 is £33,500 but only £28,500 of your dividend income will be taxed at 7.5% because the dividend allowance uses up some of your basic-rate band.)

In most cases it would not be worth becoming non-resident to avoid paying £2,138 in tax.

However, if you have a significant amount of dividend income subject to the higher rate (32.5%) or additional rate (38.1%), being non-resident becomes more attractive.

For example, let's say you are a UK resident company owner and receive dividend income of £200,000 in 2017/18 and have no other income. With this much income you will not enjoy any personal allowance but the first £5,000 of your dividend income will still be tax free thanks to the dividend allowance. You will then pay 7.5% tax on the next £28,500, 32.5% tax on the next £116,500 and 38.1% tax on the final £50,000.

Your total tax bill as a UK resident will be £59,050 which means you can potentially save £59,050 in tax if you are non-resident.

Temporary Non-Residents

Where a UK company has built up significant distributable profits it has been possible in the past to withdraw these profits as tax-free dividends during a short period of non-residence.

This tax planning opportunity is no longer available following the introduction of new anti-avoidance rules. Income from "closely controlled companies" (most small companies) will be taxed if the recipient becomes UK resident again after a temporary period of non-residence that lasts for five years or less.

This anti-avoidance rule does not apply to "post-departure trade profits". If your company makes profits while you are non-resident, dividends that are paid out of these profits will not be taxed when you return to the UK.

Post-departure trade profits are trade profits that arise in an accounting period (financial year) that begins after your period of temporary non-residence has started.

The anti-avoidance rules do not apply to employment and self-employment earnings or regular investment income, for example, dividends from stock market companies and bank interest.

Furthermore, the anti-avoidance rule will only apply where an individual has been resident in four or more of the seven tax years prior to the tax year in which they become non-resident.

While it may no longer be possible for most individuals to avoid income tax by becoming non-resident for a short period, this tax planning strategy – extracting dividends from your company after you become non-UK resident – can still work if you decide to leave the UK permanently.

Dividend Income from ISAs

If you have money in ISAs and then go abroad, you cannot continue putting money in (unless you are a Crown employee working overseas or their spouse). However, you can keep your existing ISA investments and your income (interest and dividends) and capital gains will not be subject to UK tax.

Real Estate Investment Trusts

A real estate investment trust (REIT) may pay dividends as either a property income distribution (PID) or a normal dividend or a combination of both. PIDs are taxed at normal income tax rates (20%, 40% or 45%).

PIDs are taxed as property letting income separate from any other property letting business. The gross amount is subject to tax with a credit for the 20% basic-rate tax deducted at source. PIDs are declared in Box 17 of your tax return and the tax withheld is entered in Box 19.

Non-residents cannot apply to have their PIDs paid gross with no tax deducted. However, investors may be able to claim repayment of some or all of that tax depending on the terms of the relevant double taxation treaty.

Overseas Tax

Although your dividends may escape UK tax, it is also important to consider the overseas tax implications.

It is possible that no overseas tax will be payable if you live in a tax haven or a country that does not tax foreign (i.e. UK) income (see Chapter 20). In other words, it is possible that your dividends will escape both UK tax and overseas tax. However, it is also possible that your UK dividends will be fully taxed in the country you move to and the tax could be greater than the tax you would pay as a UK resident.

You also have to be careful if you have income from ISAs. Just because your ISA income is tax free in the UK doesn't mean it will be tax free in your new country of residence.

Double Tax Treaties

Finally, as with all tax planning that involves two countries (in this case the country where the income arises and the country where you live), it may be necessary to take account of any relevant double tax treaty. A double tax treaty may reduce the amount of tax payable under the two countries' domestic tax laws.

Chapter 16

How to Pay Less Tax on UK Interest Income

If you are non-UK resident any interest you earn from *overseas bank accounts* is exempt from UK income tax.

Interest from *UK bank accounts* is taxable but in practice most non-residents will not have to pay any UK income tax.

This is because, if you don't have very much other UK income (e.g. rental income and pension income), your interest will be covered by your personal allowance (£11,500 for 2017/18) or the £5,000 starting rate band.

If your other UK income uses up your personal allowance and starting rate band, some or all of your interest income may still be tax free thanks to the new personal savings allowance. This allows you to earn up to £1,000 of tax-free interest income if you're a basic-rate taxpayer and up to £500 if you're a higher-rate taxpayer (additional-rate taxpayers get nothing).

Your interest income may also be tax free under the disregarded income calculation (see Chapter 15). This allows you to enjoy tax free interest, dividends and certain other types of income if, despite having your personal allowance taken away, this produces a lower overall tax bill.

Since 6 April 2016 banks no longer have to deduct tax from interest payments and, as a result, non-residents no longer have to complete form R105 to have their interest paid gross.

Exporting Your Cash

If you do expect to suffer some sort of tax sting because you have UK interest income it's important to point out that money held in bank accounts is arguably the most portable asset of all. It is usually relatively simple for non-residents to remove their savings from the UK taxman's clutches by putting them in an overseas bank account.

Most reputable UK banks offer offshore bank accounts which allow you to keep your money in a variety of different currencies. They are often based in low-tax jurisdictions such as the Channel Islands and the Isle of Man.

If you withdraw your savings from UK banks there may, however, be other non-tax penalties, for example if your cash is invested in some sort of fixed term deposit and you make an early withdrawal.

Although you may decide to take most of your cash out of the country, many non-residents still keep a UK bank account and credit card for all sorts of practical reasons (for example to receive payments from the UK or in anticipation of returning).

Interest from Government Bonds

If you are non-resident interest payments on UK Government securities issued on FOTRA terms (Free of Tax to Residents Abroad) are exempt from UK income tax. The exemption does not apply where the interest is received as part of a trade carried on in the UK.

Since 6 April 1998 all UK Government securities have FOTRA status and all registered gilts generally pay interest without any tax being deducted.

Interest from ISAs

You also have to be careful if you have income from ISAs. Just because your ISA income is tax free in the UK doesn't mean it will be tax free in your new country of residence. For example, the Isle of Man Government specifically states in its tax return booklet that "this tax-free status does not apply in the Isle of Man and you should declare any income from these products".

Overseas Tax

Although your interest may escape UK tax, it is also important to consider the overseas tax implications. It is possible that no overseas tax will be payable if you live in a tax haven or a country that does not tax foreign income. See Chapter 20 for more information. In other words, it is possible that your interest income will escape both UK tax and overseas tax.

However, it is also possible that your interest income will be fully taxed in the country you move to and the tax could be greater than the tax you would pay as a UK resident.

Double Tax Treaties

If there is a double tax treaty between the UK and your new country of residence, it may limit the amount of tax HMRC can levy on your interest income.

The current *Model OECD Tax Convention* states that interest income can be taxed in the country where it arises and the country where you are resident. However, in the country where the interest arises (the UK if you have a UK bank account) tax cannot exceed 10%.

In practice, not all tax treaties are the same. Some provide full relief from UK tax, some provide no relief at all from UK tax and others limit the UK tax charge to, say 10-15%.

For example, the UK-France tax treaty says that only the country where you are resident can tax your interest income. So if you live in France but receive interest income from the UK, the income will only be taxed in France.

Other countries where the tax treaty provides for full relief from UK tax on interest income include Denmark, Germany, Hong Kong, Hungary, Iceland, Ireland, Kuwait, the Netherlands, Norway, Qatar, Russia, South Africa, Sweden, Switzerland and the United States.

Other double tax treaties provide no relief or partial relief from UK tax on interest income. Those tax treaties that provide partial tax relief typically limit the UK tax charge to 10-15%. For example, the UK-Australia tax treaty provides for a maximum tax charge of 10%.

(Those who hold Australian temporary resident visas enjoy special tax concessions from the Australian Government and do not have to pay any Australian tax on their foreign investment income. Tax relief under the double tax convention does not apply to the extent that income or gains are exempt from tax in Australia.)

Chapter 17

How to Pay Less Tax on UK Pensions

If you are non-UK resident you will not pay any UK tax on your *overseas* pensions, i.e. pensions from sources outside the UK.

Of course, most UK taxpayers only have UK pensions. How will your UK pensions be taxed when you become non-resident?

According to HMRC, "When you are not UK resident you are liable to UK tax on most pensions from sources in the UK."

In practice many UK pensions are actually exempt from UK tax. This is because, under the terms of most double tax treaties, only the country where you live can tax your pension income. This is good news if you move to a country with low tax rates.

Government pensions are an exception. Tax is usually only payable in the UK, with no tax payable overseas.

Please note every double tax agreement is different. If you're thinking of becoming non-UK resident, it's important to understand how the tax treaty, if one exists, between the UK and the country you're moving to will affect your personal tax situation.

Government Pensions

The Government Service Article (Article 19) of the current OECD Model Tax Convention states that:

"pensions and other similar remuneration paid by, or out of funds created by, a Contracting State or a political subdivision or a local authority thereof to an individual in respect of services rendered to that State or subdivision or authority shall be taxable only in that State. However, such pensions and other similar remuneration shall be taxable only in the other Contracting State if the individual is a resident of, and a national of, that State."

So if you're a former Government employee (e.g. a civil servant) or local authority employee and live overseas your pension will only be taxed in the UK.

But if you're a national of the overseas country, the right to tax the pension is transferred from the UK to the overseas country.

Not every double taxation agreement has these clauses, so it's important to check the relevant treaty.

It can be quite tax efficient to have some of your income taxed exclusively in the UK and some of your income taxed exclusively in another country. This means you may get to enjoy two personal allowances and two low-tax income bands.

Example

Maria worked as a civil servant for many years and receives a pension of £30,000. She also earns £30,000 working part time. Her income tax bill in 2017/18 is £12,700.

To keep things simple we will assume that she moves to a country that has identical tax rates to the UK and the tax treaty gives the UK the exclusive right to tax her Government pension. She earns the same amount working part time overseas.

She now has £30,000 taxed in each country, i.e. two personal allowances and two basic-rate bands. Her total tax bill falls to £7,400 – a tax saving of £5,300.

What is a Government Pension?

For starters, please note that the state pension is not a Government pension. Government pensions are, generally speaking those paid to former employees of:

- The UK Government (e.g. the Civil Service)

- A local authority or other public body in the UK (e.g. Police pensions and Council pensions)

Under some tax treaties local authority pensions are not

considered Government pensions and are exempt from UK tax, along with regular occupational pensions.

For more information about specific public sector pensions go to:

www.gov.uk/hmrc-internal-manuals/international-manual/intm343040

The NHS pension is not classed as a Government pension if it is paid by CAPITA or the Paymaster Generals office. If the NHS pension is paid by a local authority, it is classed as a Government pension.

Government Pensions – What the Tax Treaties Say

If you live in the following countries your UK Government pension will be exempt from UK tax: Albania, Argentina, Australia (temporary residents excluded), Canada, Cyprus, Fiji, Guernsey, the Isle of Man, Jersey, the Netherlands, New Zealand, Papua New Guinea, and Tunisia.

In other words, if you live in the Isle of Man your UK Government pension will only be taxed in the Isle of Man.

Holders of Australian Temporary Resident visas do not have to pay tax in Australia on their foreign income (with the exception of employment income). Thus to prevent their pensions being tax exempt in both the UK and Australia the income is taxed in the UK.

Under many other double tax treaties UK Government pensions are exempt from UK tax, provided you are both a **resident and national** of the other overseas country. These include: Bahrain, Barbados, Belgium, Bolivia, Bosnia-Herzegovina, Botswana, Bulgaria, China, Croatia, Czech Republic, Denmark, Estonia, Ethiopia, Finland, France (non-UK nationals only), Georgia, Germany, Ghana, Guyana, Iceland, Indonesia, Ireland, Italy, Japan, Jordan, Kazakhstan, Korea, Kosovo, Kuwait, Latvia, Lesotho, Libya, Lithuania, Macedonia, Malaysia, Malta, Mexico, Moldova, Mongolia, Montenegro, Norway, Oman, Pakistan, Poland, Qatar, Russia, Saudi Arabia, Serbia, Singapore, Slovakia, Slovenia, South Africa, Spain, Sweden, Switzerland, Taiwan, Tajikistan, Thailand, Trinidad & Tobago, Turkey, Turkmenistan, Uganda, Ukraine, USA, Uzbekistan, Vietnam, Zambia and Zimbabwe.

In other words, if you live in South Africa and are also a South African national your UK Government pension will only be taxed in South Africa.

In some countries UK Government pensions are exempt from UK tax as long as you are a national of that country and **not a UK national**, including: Austria, Bangladesh, Egypt, Greece, Hungary, Mauritius, Romania, and Sri Lanka.

If you live in the Cayman Islands your UK Government pension will not be taxed in the UK if you have been continuously resident in the Cayman Islands either:

- For a period of 6 years immediately before your pension payments start

- For a period of 6 years immediately before the related employment starts

I highlight the Cayman Islands because it is one of the best known tax havens – the island has no income tax. So if your pension is exempt from UK tax under the double tax treaty, it will be completely tax free.

Occupational Pensions and State Pensions

Many tax treaties state that private sector occupational pensions, state pensions and certain other types of pension are exempt from UK tax, i.e. they are only taxed in the overseas country where you live.

However, tax treaties vary considerably. For example, some do not exempt state pensions from UK tax.

Having your UK pension taxed overseas only could be extremely tax efficient if the country you move to has lower tax rates than the UK. For example, in Cyprus foreign pensions are only taxed at 5% (with the first €3,420 exempt from tax).

The following is a list of countries where UK pensions (excluding Government pensions) are exempt from UK tax and some of the conditions that apply:

Country	Conditions
Albania	
Antigua & Barbuda	If subject to tax there
Argentina	No relief for state pension
Armenia	
Australia	Excludes temporary resident visas
Austria	
Bangladesh	No relief for state pension
Barbados	
Belarus	
Belgium	If first payments before 1/1/2014
Belize	If subject to tax there
Bolivia	
Bosnia-Herzegovina	
Botswana	If subject to tax there No relief for state pension
British Virgin Islands	If you have a certificate of residence and after 10 years non-UK residence
Brunei	If subject to tax there
Bulgaria	If subject to tax there, no relief for state pension
Canada	
Cayman Islands	If Cayman resident for 6 years before commencement of pension
China	
Croatia	
Cyprus	If subject to tax there
Czech Republic	
Egypt	
Estonia	
Falkland Islands	If subject to tax there
Faroes	No relief for state pension
Fiji	No relief for state pension
France	
Georgia	
Germany	If less than 15 years contributions No relief for state pension
Ghana	If subject to tax there
Greece	If subject to tax there
Grenada	If subject to tax there
Guernsey	
Guyana	
Hungary	

Country	Conditions
India	
Ireland	
Isle of Man	
Israel	If subject to tax there
Italy	
Ivory Coast	
Jamaica	If subject to tax there
Japan	
Jersey	
Kazakhstan	
Kiribati	If subject to tax there
Korea	
Kosovo	
Kuwait	If subject to tax there
Latvia	
Lesotho	
Lithuania	
Luxembourg	No relief for state pension
Macedonia	
Malawi	If subject to tax there
Malaysia	No relief for state pension
Malta	State pension only relievable if subject to tax in Malta
Mauritius	State pension only relievable if subject to tax in Mauritius
Mexico	No relief for state pension
Moldova	
Mongolia	No relief for state pension
Montenegro	
Morocco	State pension only relievable if subject to tax in Morocco
Namibia	If subject to tax there
Netherlands	
New Zealand	
Norway	
Oman	If subject to tax there
Pakistan	No relief for state pension
Papua New Guinea	If subject to tax there
Philippines	No relief for state pension or purchased annuities
Poland	
Portugal	State pension only relievable if subject to tax in Portugal

Country	Conditions
Qatar	No relief for state pension
Romania	
Russia	
St Kitts & Nevis	If subject to tax there
Saudi Arabia	
Serbia	
Sierra Leone	If subject to tax there
Singapore	If subject to tax there
Slovak Republic	
Slovenia	
Solomon Islands	If subject to tax there
South Africa	No relief for state pension
Spain	
Sri Lanka	If subject to tax there
Swaziland	
Switzerland	
Taiwan	If subject to tax there
	No relief for state pension
Tajikistan	
Trinidad & Tobago	No relief for state pension
Tunisia	If subject to tax there
Turkey	
Turkmenistan	
Tuvalu	If subject to tax there
Uganda	
Ukraine	
USA	
Uzbekistan	
Vietnam	
Zambia	No relief for state pension

Notice the phrase "If subject to tax there". This means your UK pension will only be exempt from UK tax if it is subject to tax in the country concerned. Some of the tax treaties that have this clause are with tax havens (e.g. Brunei and St Kitts). If you live in one, your pension will presumably still be taxed in the UK (because there is no income tax in those countries).

The UK's tax treaties with certain other tax havens (e.g. the British Virgin Islands, the Cayman Islands, and Qatar) do not call for your pension to be taxed in those territories, so it may in certain circumstances be possible to enjoy a tax-free pension if you live in those places.

Applying for Tax Treaty Exemptions

Occupational and private pensions will normally have tax deducted at source by the pension provider under PAYE. The Department for Work and Pensions does not deduct tax from your state pension, but it is taxable income. Instead, the PAYE tax code for your private or occupational pension will normally be adjusted so that part of your tax-free personal allowance is allocated against your state pension, which reduces the personal allowance available for your other income.

If you have more than one occupational or private pension, your personal allowance is usually allocated against the main pension. Any additional pensions are normally taxed at 20% using a BR (basic rate) code.

If you are entitled to receive your UK pension free of UK tax you must make a claim to have the tax deductions stopped. To ask HMRC to stop deducting tax at source, or to request a refund of tax already deducted, you should complete Form DT-Individual:

www.gov.uk/government/publications/double-taxation-treaty-relief-form-dt-individual

The tax office in the relevant overseas country will stamp the form and return it to you to forward to HMRC.

Specific claim forms are available for the following countries:

- Australia
- Canada
- France
- Germany
- Ireland
- Japan
- New Zealand
- Netherlands
- South Africa
- Spain
- Sweden
- Switzerland
- United States of America

To obtain the relevant form go to:

www.gov.uk/government/collections/living-and-working-abroad-and-offshore-forms

Temporary Non-Residents

Under the current UK pension rules once you're old enough you can withdraw as much cash as you like from your pension savings. Most of the income you withdraw will, however, be subject to UK income tax.

The temporary non-residence anti-avoidance rules prevent people from leaving the country, withdrawing all their pension savings and paying much less tax in some other country than they would in the UK.

If you become UK resident again within five years, your pension income could be subject to UK tax again, if your withdrawals exceeded £100,000.

State Pensions – Further Issues

The state pension is taxable income but relief from UK income tax is available under the terms of many double tax treaties.

Your state pension may also be exempt from UK tax under the "disregarded income" calculation (see Chapter 15). This allows you to enjoy tax-free interest, dividends, state pension and certain other types of income if, despite having your personal allowance taken away, this produces a lower overall tax bill.

Some expats receive a raw deal when it comes to annual increases in their state pension. You will only receive annual increases if you live in:

- The European Economic Area (EEA) and Switzerland
- Countries that have a social security agreement with the UK (and the agreement allows for annual pension increases)

If you live outside those areas, you won't be entitled to any increase in your state pension. However, if you return to live in the UK, your state pension will be increased to current levels.

To find out which countries have a social security agreement with the UK, follow the link on this page:

www.gov.uk/new-state-pension/living-and-working-overseas

Apparently over 500,000 expats living in countries such as Australia, Canada, New Zealand and South Africa are affected by this state pension freeze.

Voluntary National Insurance Contributions

When you live abroad you can make voluntary national insurance contributions to make up any gaps in your national insurance record. This will allow you to receive a bigger state pension.

There are two types of voluntary contribution: Class 2 and Class 3.

Class 2 contributions are much cheaper (£148 in 2017/18) but are to be abolished from April 2018. As a result, anyone who lives overseas and wants to increase their state pension will have to pay Class 3 contributions. The current cost is £741 (2017/18).

Although Class 3 contributions are more expensive, many commentators believe they will still be worth paying. This is because you only have to draw your state pension for just a few years to fully recover the cost.

You can pay Class 3 contributions if:

- You have lived in the UK for a continuous three-year period at any time before the period for which contributions are to be paid. (If you have lived or worked in another EEA country or in Turkey, time spent there might help you to meet this condition), or

- Before you went abroad, you paid a set amount in national insurance contributions for three years or more (this will be checked when you ask to pay Class 3 contributions).

Overseas Tax

Although your pension may escape UK tax, it is also important to consider the overseas tax implications.

You could end up paying more tax or less tax than you would in the UK – it all hinges on where you decide to live.

Couples may be able to cut their tax bills significantly by moving to a country that has lower tax rates and/or lets them split their pension income – often referred to as joint assessment.

For example, in the Isle of Man, not only are tax rates lower than in the UK (the top tax rate is 20%), but married couples can elect to be taxed jointly, which results in a doubling up of the personal allowance and 10% tax band.

Example

Jack lives in the Isle of Man and receives pension income of £50,000 from the UK. His wife Jill has no income. Under the double tax agreement with the UK, Jack's pension is only taxed in the Isle of Man and the couple decide to be assessed jointly to double up their personal allowances and 10% tax bands. As a result income tax is payable as follows on Jack's pension income in 2017/18:

- *First £25,000   0%*
- *Next £13,000   10%*
- *Final £12,000   20%*

With joint assessment the couple's tax bill is £3,700. If the couple lived in the UK all the income would be taxed in Jack's hands and Jill's personal allowance would be wasted. The total tax bill would be £8,700. The couple save income tax of £5,000 per year in the Isle of Man.

Pension Lump Sums

UK residents can take 25% of their pension savings as a tax-free lump sum. In some countries these payments are taxable, which means you may be better off taking your lump sum *before* you leave the UK, although this is not always tax efficient.

For example, in France lump sums from UK pensions are taxed but it is possible to opt for a fixed tax rate of 7.5% (with a 10% deduction). Some commentators on French tax matters say that your whole pension fund can be taxed at this special rate (including the amount that would be fully taxed in the UK) but only if you take your whole pension fund in one go.

There may also be social charges of 7.4% but these are not payable if you are not affiliated to the French health system, for example if you hold Form S1.

Lump sums are also taxed in Spain, although the tax is limited to the fund's *investment growth* and not your initial contributions.

Pension Contributions when Non-UK Resident

After you become non-UK resident you can continue to make contributions to a UK pension scheme and enjoy tax relief for a limited period.

The rules say that tax relief is available as long as you were UK resident at some point during the immediately preceding five tax years and also when you joined the pension scheme.

Thus you can continue to make UK pension contributions for up to five tax years after the tax year in which you become non-resident.

If you do not have a UK salary or other "relevant UK earnings" (which is likely if you are non-resident) your contributions will be capped at £3,600 per year – you contribute £2,880 and the taxman will contribute £720.

Tax relief is generally only available if your contributions are paid to a relief at source pension scheme (generally speaking a personal pension).

Double Tax Treaties and Pension Contributions

If you work in one country you generally cannot contribute to a pension in another country and enjoy tax relief in the country where you work.

However, some of the UK's double tax treaties allow non-resident employees to make contributions to a UK pension scheme and enjoy tax relief in the country where they are working.

This could appeal to those who do not intend to emigrate permanently and wish to keep their retirement savings in one pot in the UK.

There are often conditions, for example you must not be resident in the new country before you start working there.

The contributions will be subject to the pension contribution limits and rules that apply in the country where you are working.

Countries where this is possible include Canada (for 60 months), Denmark (if you work for the same employer as in the UK), France, Ireland (if same employer), South Africa and the USA.

Chapter 18

QROPs: Recent Tax Changes

If you emigrate you can keep your pension savings in the UK, where they will continue to grow tax free until you start withdrawing money (from age 55 at present).

Alternatively, you can transfer your pension pot overseas to a Qualifying Recognised Overseas Pension Scheme (QROPS).

Why do this? A few years ago financial advisors promoted QROPS on the basis that all your money could be taken as a tax-free lump sum, compared with the 25% tax-free lump sum available to UK residents.

After this rule was tightened the main tax benefit seemed to be avoiding death taxes. In the UK there used to be a 55% tax on pension savings left to relatives in certain circumstances, whereas financial advisors promoting QROPS argued that your savings could be paid as a tax-free lump sum to your beneficiaries.

The 55% UK death tax has now been abolished which means your beneficiaries can now inherit all your pension savings without any tax being deducted, at least initially. In many cases they will, however, still have to pay income tax on any money they withdraw, although this is a lot better than paying tax at 55%.

QROPS were also lauded for allowing bigger income withdrawals than UK pensions. This benefit has now disappeared following the recent liberalisation of UK pensions – UK retirees can now withdraw as much money from their pensions as they like.

QROPS have also been promoted for their ability to protect you from exchange rate fluctuations (for example, if you retire somewhere in Europe you may want your pension denominated in Euros) and for their ability to protect you from the lifetime allowance cap on pension savings and future adverse changes to UK pensions legislation.

Financial advisors have also promoted QROPs on the grounds that they could help you save income tax. For example, in the UAE there is no tax on pension income but because there is no double tax agreement between the UAE and the UK, income from a UK pension would remain taxable in the UK. By contrast, Malta does have a double tax agreement with the UAE, so by transferring a UK pension to a Malta QROPS, advisors argued it would be possible to pay no tax on your pension income in the UAE.

However, in the March 2017 Budget the Government has introduced new rules which will make it much harder to enjoy big income tax savings using a QROPS (see below).

QROPS have been aggressively marketed by some firms of financial advisors. However, the benefits of these schemes over traditional UK pensions have been significantly reduced over time due to a tightening of the QROPS rules and a relaxation of the rules applying to UK pensions.

While QROPS may still offer some benefits in certain circumstances, in other cases non-residents may be better off keeping their UK pensions in place.

When QROPS May Be a Bad Idea

People who should possibly not transfer their pension pots to a QROPS include:

- **Members of final salary pension schemes**. These are the Rolls Royce of pensions because there is no investment risk for the member – your pension is based on your salary rather than how well your investments perform. This benefit will be lost if you switch to a QROPS. (Note, at the time of writing, some financial advisors are currently recommending transfers out of final salary schemes because the transfer values are so generous.)

- **Temporary emigrants**. If you think you'll return to the UK one day, you may be better off leaving your pension savings here.

- **Those with small pension pots**. QROPS fees are usually higher than those of UK schemes (sometimes considerably higher) and some of the benefits are only enjoyed by individuals with significant pension savings.

Changes Announced in March 2017

If you emigrate to, say, New Zealand you may wish to transfer your pension to a QROPS in New Zealand. However, you don't have to transfer your pension to a QROPS in the country you move to. The so-called "third-party QROPS" have been heavily promoted by financial advisors and are based in countries like Malta, Gibraltar and the Isle of Man.

However, using a third party QROPS may become a lot less attractive following changes announced in the March 2017 Budget.

From 9 March 2017 certain transfers to and from a QROPS will be liable to a 25% tax charge called the overseas transfer charge.

Where a transfer is not subject to the overseas transfer charge it could be taxed later on. This will happen if, within five full tax years after the transfer, you fail to still meet the conditions which originally made the transfer tax free.

The 25% overseas transfer charge will be payable unless you meet at least one of the following five conditions:

- You are resident in the same country in which the QROPS receiving the transfer is established.

- You are resident in an EEA country and the QROPS is established in a country within the EEA.

- The QROPS is set up by an international organisation for the purpose of providing benefits for or in respect of past service as an employee of the organisation and the member is an employee of that international organisation.

- The QROPS is an overseas public service pension scheme and you are employed by one of the employer's participating in the scheme.

- The QROPS is an occupational pension scheme sponsored by your employer.

If you are resident in the country where the QROPS is established or resident in an EEA country and the QROPS is established in an EEA country, but after the transfer takes place your circumstances change and neither of these conditions is met, the overseas transfer charge will become payable.

This only applies if the change of circumstances takes place within the relevant period of five full tax years from the date of the original transfer from the registered pension scheme to the QROPS.

Payments out of funds transferred to a QROPS on or after 6 April 2017 will be subject to UK tax rules for five tax years after the date of transfer, regardless of where the individual is resident.

Which QROPS Will Be Affected?

Australia and New Zealand are popular destinations. If you move to Australia and use an Australian QROPS or move to New Zealand and use a New Zealand QROPS you will not be subject to the new 25% overseas transfer charge.

If you use a Malta QROPS and live in the EEA you will also not be subject to the overseas transfer charge because Malta is an EEA country.

In most other cases if you live in a country different to where your QROPS is established, you will be subject to the new 25% charge, for example, if you use an Isle of Man or Gibraltar QROPS but live in a different country.

Other QROPS Dangers

Overseas pension schemes must comply with HMRC rules, otherwise your pension transfer could be subject to a hefty 55% unauthorised payment charge.

HMRC publishes a list of recognised pension schemes that can be found by typing "recognised overseas pension schemes" into Google. In recent years a significant number of pension schemes have been removed from the list. For example, in 2015 HMRC culled a huge number of Australian schemes because they were allowing members to access their pension savings before reaching the UK's minimum retirement age of 55.

It's important to point out that, even if a pension scheme appears on this list, this does not mean the scheme has been officially approved by HMRC. HMRC cannot guarantee that transfers to these schemes will escape the unauthorised payment charge. In fact, HMRC now refers to QROPS only as ROPS having removed the word "Qualifying" to drive home the message that it could take action against such schemes in the future.

Furthermore, from 6 April 2017 the requirements to be a ROPS are changing with HMRC publishing a revised list on 18 April 2017.

A summary of the changes can be found here:

www.gov.uk/government/publications/pension-tax-for-overseas-pensions

Chapter 19

How to Pay Less Tax on Employment Income

If you are non-resident there is no UK tax payable on salary you receive for doing work outside the UK. It doesn't matter if you work for a UK employer or are paid in the UK.

If your overseas job starts during the tax year you may be taxed as a UK resident for the first part of the year and non-resident for the second part of the year.

If you have an overseas job, you may be subject to UK tax for duties performed in the UK, unless they are "merely incidental" to your overseas job.

UK tax may be payable on work carried out in the UK even though you have a full-time overseas job and spend a relatively small amount of time working in the UK (although it may be possible to claim exemption from UK tax under a double tax agreement).

If you expect to become non-resident you have to complete form P85. This form asks you to provide details of your overseas job, if you have one, and how much time you expect to spend working in the UK, if any.

If you will remain on a UK payroll when you are non-resident HMRC will issue a no tax (NT) PAYE code so that no UK income tax is deducted from your pay (although national insurance may remain payable).

However, if some of your duties will be performed in the UK, despite being non-resident, HMRC will tell you how much tax should be deducted based on the proportion of time you spend working in the UK.

Civil Servants and Military Personnel

These groups are treated as performing all their duties in the UK and are therefore subject to UK tax.

Merely Incidental Duties

If you are non-resident and do some work in the UK there is no UK tax payable if the work you do is merely incidental to your overseas job.

Each case is different but HMRC has indicated that if the work done in the UK is the same or of similar importance to the work you do overseas, then it is NOT merely incidental.

Activities that may be regarded as merely incidental include:

- Arranging meetings and travel
- Providing feedback on employee performance or business results – as long as this is not one of your core duties
- Providing input on certain staff matters, provided you do not have a management role in the business
- Reading generic business emails

For example, if you work for an overseas subsidiary of a UK company and occasionally visit the UK headquarters merely to present reports and take instructions (but you do not have any control over the overseas activities), these duties are regarded as merely incidental to your overseas duties.

If an employee of an overseas company receives an email about the company's results for the year while visiting the UK and is not required to take any further action or provide feedback, reading the email is merely incidental to his overseas duties. If the employee helped produce the results or has to provide feedback, reading the email is not a merely incidental duty.

Let's take another example. An employee of an international bank based in a city in mainland Europe, visits a UK branch of the bank. Whilst in the UK branch, the employee responds to an investment enquiry sent by email from a customer of the bank in Germany.

This represents a duty of his employment in Europe and by answering the email from the UK he performs a duty that is directly related to his duties in Europe. Consequently this cannot be a "merely incidental" duty.

Duties that are Not Merely Incidental:

These include:

- Providing guidance or instructions to colleagues
- Reporting on performance/business results if these are one of your core duties
- Analysing information to produce results or recommendations that can be sent to colleagues
- Discussions or meetings with clients, colleagues, directors and shareholders (including by telephone)
- Preparation work or follow-up work related to these discussions or meetings
- Any activities that are part of your contractual duties

Attending Directors' Meetings

Attending board meetings is a core function of a company director. Thus, attending board meetings cannot be a "merely incidental" duty, regardless of the fact that the director does not normally attend meetings in person.

Tax Repayments

When you become non-resident, there's a good chance you'll be entitled to a tax refund. This is because, under PAYE, your monthly tax deduction assumes that you will earn the same income for the *entire tax year*.

For example, if your salary is £36,000, your monthly tax deduction will be around £400. If you become non-resident half way through the tax year your UK income for the year will be £18,000, not £36,000, and you'll be entitled to a tax refund of over £1,000.

A repayment can be obtained by submitting your P45 (the form you get when you leave your job) along with your P85. You may have to complete a tax return before receiving a refund. If you are not leaving your job (i.e. you will be working for the same employer overseas) you will not receive a P45 and should ask your employer for a letter confirming how much you've earned to date and how much UK tax has been deducted from your salary.

Relocation Costs

If your employer helps you move home, up to £8,000 of expenses can be reimbursed tax free (plus a further £8,000 if you return to the UK).

The exemption is generally not available if your employer pays you a cash lump sum to do with as you like.

Expenses that qualify include: Costs incurred selling your old home and buying your new one (legal fees, estate agent's fees, loan arrangement and redemption fees, stamp duty), interest on bridging loans (used to redeem the loan on your old home or to buy your new home), removal costs, temporary accommodation costs at the new location (if you leave your old home before you occupy your new one), certain travel costs, and the cost of replacing domestic goods like carpets, curtains and cookers, if the ones in your old home are unsuitable for your new home.

Some costs paid by your employer are not exempt including mortgage payments for your existing home, mail re-direction, council tax, compensation paid for any loss on the sale of your home or any other losses (e.g. school fees payable for giving insufficient notice to the school).

Double Tax Treaties

If you are non-UK resident and your employer sends you to the UK to work for less than six months, you may be exempt from paying UK tax on your employment income under the terms of a double tax treaty. Most of the UK's double tax treaties contain a clause that protects short-term foreign workers from local taxes (although the terms of double tax treaties vary).

Typically, to qualify for tax relief if you work in the UK temporarily you must meet the following conditions:

- **The 183 Day Rule.** Some tax treaties state that you must not be present in the UK for more than 183 days in the tax year concerned. More recent tax treaties have a much tighter test and state that you must not be present in the UK for more than 183 days in any 12 month period that begins or ends in the tax year concerned.

- **Non-Resident Employer.** Your salary must be paid by an employer who is not UK resident. If you work at a UK business during your visit it is possible that the UK business will be treated as your employer if that business is, in practice, acting as your employer. As a result your income will not be exempt from UK tax.

- **Permanent establishment**. Your salary must not be paid by a permanent establishment which your employer has in the UK.

Of course, this exemption works the other way as well: if you are UK resident and work overseas for less than six months you may be exempt from overseas tax.

National Insurance

Many countries levy social security contributions similar to UK national insurance. If you work abroad you may remain subject to UK national insurance or you may have to make contributions in the country where you live. It all depends on where you go, for how long and whether you work for a UK or foreign employer.

The EEA or Switzerland

The general rule is you pay social security contributions in the country where you work. For example, if you work for a foreign employer or intend to leave the UK permanently you will not be required to pay UK national insurance (although you can pay voluntary contributions to protect your state pension).

However, there are some exceptions for short-term workers and certain types of workers (e.g. those who normally work in more than one country, transport workers, and government employees). For example, if you are an EEA national and your UK employer sends you to work in an EEA country or Switzerland for a period expected to last no more than two years, you will usually continue to pay UK national insurance.

Before you go abroad your employer should apply to HMRC for a Portable Document A1 which means you will not have to pay social security contributions in the country where you work.

If you are not an EEA national and your UK employer sends you to work in an EEA country for a period expected to last no more than a year, you will usually continue to pay UK national insurance.

Before you go abroad your employer should apply to HMRC for a form E101 which means you will not have to pay social security contributions in the country where you work. If the work lasts longer you can apply for a 12 month extension (form E102).

Similar rules apply to self-employed individuals who work temporarily in the EEA or Switzerland.

For the purposes of the EU social security rules, you are treated as being resident in the country in which you are 'habitually resident'. This is based on an assessment of the facts but will usually be the country you normally live in and where you have your centre of interests.

Countries with Social Security Agreements

Again, the general rule is that you pay social security contributions in the country where you work. For example, if you work for a foreign employer or intend to leave the UK permanently you will not be required to pay UK national insurance.

The UK has social security agreements with a number of countries including Barbados, Bermuda, Bosnia and Herzegovina, Canada, the Isle of Man, Israel, Jamaica, Japan, Jersey and Guernsey, Kosovo, Macedonia, Mauritius, Montenegro, New Zealand, the Philippines, Serbia, Turkey, and the USA.

Under these agreements, if your posting is only expected to last for a certain length of time you and your employer will be required to keep paying UK national insurance.

The time periods vary from country to country:

- Barbados   3 years
- Bermuda   12 months
- Canada   5 years
- Isle of Man   Limited agreement
- Israel   2 years
- Jamaica   3 years
- Japan   5 years
- Jersey   3 years
- Guernsey   3 years
- Mauritius   2 years
- Philippines   3 years
- Turkey   3 years
- USA   5 years

Your employer should obtain a certificate of continuing liability to prevent contributions being paid in the other country.

Some special groups (e.g. aircrew, civil servants and people who normally work in both countries) may be subject to special provisions, typically paying contributions in their home country.

Similar rules apply to self-employed individuals. You pay contributions in the country where you work but there are exceptions for people normally self-employed in the UK who do business in a reciprocal agreement country. You should apply to HMRC for a certificate of continuing liability to avoid paying contributions in the other country.

Other Countries

The general rule is you will have to pay national insurance in the country where you are working. However, you will be required to pay UK national insurance for the first 52 weeks if:

- Your employer has a place of business in the UK, and
- You are ordinarily resident in the UK
- You were UK resident immediately before working abroad.

This may be on top of social security contributions in the country where you are working.

Note that the country where you are resident for tax purposes is not necessarily the same as the country where you are resident and ordinarily resident for national insurance.

You are ordinarily resident in a country if it is where you are settled and normally live, apart from temporary absences. Factors such as where your partner and children live and whether you have a UK home are taken into account.

For more information go to:

www.gov.uk/government/publications/social-security-abroad-ni38

Chapter 20

Overseas Income Tax

So far we've looked at how much UK tax is payable on your UK income when you become non-resident.

Of course, you may also have to pay tax in the country you move to – this point has been made repeatedly in the previous chapters.

This chapter provides a brief overview of how your UK income may be taxed overseas. In particular, we will focus on countries that have low tax rates or offer special concessions for immigrants who have overseas (i.e. UK) income.

Tax Havens

If you move to a "tax haven" (i.e. a country that doesn't levy any income tax at all) you do not have to worry about paying any additional tax on your UK income and you do not have to worry about paying any tax on the income you generate inside that country (e.g. your salary if you work there):

Countries that have no personal income tax include:

- Anguilla
- Bahamas
- Bahrain
- Bermuda
- British Virgin Islands
- Brunei
- Cayman Islands
- Kuwait
- Monaco
- Oman
- Qatar
- St Kitts and Nevis
- Saudi Arabia
- Turks & Caicos
- United Arab Emirates

Although the above countries do not, strictly speaking, levy personal income tax, some of them do impose other taxes on individuals, in particular those who are employed or self employed.

For example, in Qatar sole traders are subject to corporate income tax on Qatari-source income. The general rate is 10%.

In Saudi Arabia self-employed foreign professionals and consultants pay 20% income tax on profits derived from activities in Saudi Arabia.

In the Bahamas self-employed people pay an annual business licence fee of up to 1% of turnover.

In the British Virgin Islands there is a payroll tax paid by employers and employees. For employees the rate is 8%, although the first $10,000 is tax free. For small employers the rate is 2% and for larger ones the rate is 6%.

Low-Tax Countries

Most countries levy income tax but the rates vary considerably. Many Western European countries and other developed countries have top tax rates well in excess of 40%.

Countries that have a top tax rate of 20% or less include:

- Angola   17%
- Belarus   13%
- Bosnia-Herzegovina   10%
- Bulgaria   10%
- Czech Republic   15%
- Georgia   20%
- Guernsey   20%
- Hong Kong   15%
- Hungary   15%
- Isle of Man   20%

- Jersey — 20%
- Jordan — 20%
- Lithuania — 15%
- Macau — 12%
- Macedonia — 10%
- Mauritius — 15%
- Romania — 16%
- Russia — 13%
- Serbia — 20%
- Ukraine — 20%
- Yemen — 15%

Social Security Contributions

If you intend to work in another country it's important to find out what, if any, social security taxes are payable (like UK national insurance).

For example, in some countries like Singapore you could end up paying more in social security taxes than you do in income tax (although the overall amount of tax you will pay may still be much lower than in most European countries).

Social security taxes are usually paid by both employees and employers, so if you intend to run a business and employ people in another country, these charges could increase your costs significantly. For example, in France the employer's social security bill comes to around 50% of the employee's pay in some cases.

Even so-called tax havens levy social security taxes. For example, in the British Virgin Islands employers pay 4.5% and employees pay 4%.

Popular Destinations

Most people do not emigrate to tax havens or countries with low tax rates. The most popular destinations for UK expats, along with the highest income tax rate payable, include:

Australia	45%
United States	39.6%
Spain	48%*
Canada	54%**
Ireland	48%
France	45%***
New Zealand	33%
South Africa	41%

* Andalucia and Catalonia; lower in other regions
**Includes highest provincial tax rate (Nova Scotia)
*** Ignores social security surcharges and the exceptional tax

Although these countries have high maximum tax rates, some of them do offer tax concessions:

Australia

If you are Australian resident for tax purposes you have to pay tax on your worldwide income. You start paying 32.5% tax once your income exceeds $37,000 (roughly £23,000). The top rate is 45%.

However, if you are a "temporary resident" your foreign investment income (interest, dividends, pensions and rental income) will not be taxed in Australia. Any foreign employment income you earn will be taxed, however. Your overseas capital gains are also exempted but not gains from Australian property.

Australia has several different types of temporary resident visa for wealthy retirees, skilled workers and entrepreneurs:

www.border.gov.au/about/corporate/information/fact-sheets/47temporary-residence

Ireland

In Ireland non-domiciled individuals are entitled to use the remittance basis. This means income tax and capital gains tax is only payable on Irish source income and gains. Overseas income and gains are only taxed if they are remitted to Ireland.

For this reason some non-domiciled individuals set up separate bank accounts for income and gains accumulated before becoming resident (exempt) and income and gains that arise after becoming resident (exempt unless remitted to Ireland).

Foreign employment income can be exempt under the remittance basis for duties performed outside Ireland under a foreign contract.

Tax-Free Foreign Income

Many countries offer tax concessions for those with foreign income (e.g. UK income). Sometimes only certain individuals qualify (e.g. non-nationals) or the exemption lasts for a limited time or only applies to certain types of income. In some cases the exemption is only available for income that is kept abroad.

Table 2 contains a list of countries that do not tax foreign income and some of the conditions that apply.

The Panama Fiasco

We're not talking about the infamous "Panama Papers" here. In 2013 Panama almost committed tax haven suicide by rushing through a law to tax foreign income. Under the new law, individuals living in Panama and companies registered there would have had to pay tax on their worldwide income, instead of just their Panamanian-sourced income.

After a huge public outcry (the tax exemption is the cornerstone of the country's finance industry and the main reason many people move there) the new law was repealed.

However, this fiasco highlights the risks of moving to a country to exploit tax loopholes – favourable tax laws can be changed at the stroke of a pen.

Table 2
Countries with Favourable Tax Treatment
for Foreign Income

Country	Terms
Angola	
Belgium	Expatriate tax regime for non-Belgian executives
Botswana	
Chile	For up to 6 years
China	For up to 5 years (non-domiciled individuals only)
Costa Rica	
Dominican Republic	Excludes certain foreign investment income
Hong Kong	
India	If not ordinarily resident
Japan	Non-permanent residents, if income not remitted
Jersey	If not ordinarily resident, if income not remitted
Jordan	
Kenya	Excludes employment income and business income
Korea	Foreign nationals, if income not remitted
	Time limits apply
Lebanon	
Macau	
Malawi	
Malta	If not domiciled, if income not remitted
Malaysia	
Mauritius	If income not remitted
Namibia	
Nigeria	Exempt if in convertible currency and repatriated through domiciliary accounts
Panama	
Philippines	Resident aliens
Singapore	
Switzerland	Income from foreign business and real estate exempt but may affect tax rate
Taiwan	
Thailand	Exempt unless remitted in year earned
Zambia	
Zimbabwe	

Chapter 21

Big Brother is Watching You!

It has always been illegal to hide undeclared income in offshore bank accounts. Nowadays it is arguably impossible. The days of secret bank accounts are over.

All over the world countries are sharing more information about individuals' bank accounts and other assets in a gigantic global crack down on tax evasion. The flow of information will increase dramatically over the next couple of years.

Several years ago there was a big drive to sign "tax information exchange agreements", which allowed countries like the UK to request information held by banks and information about the ownership of companies and trusts in numerous so-called tax havens, including Liechtenstein, the Channel Islands, Gibraltar, the Isle of Man and most of the Caribbean islands (the Bahamas, Bermuda, the British Virgin Islands etc).

The problem with tax information exchange agreements is the countries generally only agreed to share information *on request* rather than *automatically*. If the UK taxman doesn't know who has offshore bank accounts and where, requesting information is much more difficult.

Automatic Information Sharing

To solve this problem governments around the world have introduced the Common Reporting Standard (CRS) which provides for the *automatic* exchange of information between countries.

Based on the US Foreign Account Tax Compliance Act (FATCA), it's a co-ordinated global attempt to force disclosure of information about income earned by individuals and other entities.

According to the OECD, 101 jurisdictions have now agreed to start automatically exchanging financial account information in September 2017 and 2018 under the Common Reporting Standard.

Countries that have signed up to the Common Reporting Standard will obtain information from their financial institutions (including account balances, income details, and information about asset sales) and send it to other signatory countries automatically on an annual basis.

The financial institutions that need to report information include banks, insurance companies, investment funds, trusts and foundations.

The end result is HMRC will automatically receive a huge amount of information on all the financial assets owned overseas by UK residents, including their bank accounts, investments and overseas structures...without having to request it.

The Common Reporting Standard comes into effect in stages. The 'early adopters' (including the EU and UK offshore centres) will start exchanging information by September 2017.

Other countries will start sharing information by September 2018.

Worldwide Disclosure Facility

Up until recently HMRC gave incentives to encourage people to come forward and clear up their tax affairs. That's no longer the case but, before automatic exchange comes into force, the Worldwide Disclosure Facility offers the chance to come forward before HMRC uses the new Common Reporting Standard data and toughens its treatment of offshore tax evaders.

The facility opened on 5 September 2016 and will run until 30 September 2018.

It does not provide immunity from prosecution but making a voluntary disclosure minimises the risk of a criminal investigation. Those who fail to make a complete or accurate disclosure could be subject to:

- A higher penalty
- Civil or criminal investigation
- Having their details published on the HMRC website

Part 3

Non-Residents: Capital Gains Tax Planning

Chapter 22

UK Capital Gains Tax

If you are UK resident you have to pay UK capital gains tax on your *worldwide* capital gains. In other words, both your UK and foreign capital gains are subject to UK capital gains tax.

So if you make a big profit selling your holiday home on the Med, you will have to pay UK capital gains tax. You may also have to pay capital gains tax in the country where the property is located.

Non-residents are generally not subject to UK capital gains tax. In other words, if you sell a UK or foreign asset after becoming non-UK resident, your profits will not be taxed in the UK. Tax may, however, be payable in another country, e.g. the country where you now live.

Although non-residents generally do not pay UK capital gains tax there are a couple of exceptions where tax is payable:

- If you realize capital gains during a period of temporary non-residence (i.e. a period of non-residence that lasts for five years or less), your gains will be taxed when you become UK resident again.

- Residential property gains that arise after 5 April 2015.

- If you are carrying on a 'trade, profession or vocation' in the UK through a branch or agency, any gains that arise from assets connected to that business will be taxable.

Temporary Non-Residence

Temporary non-residence is covered in Chapters 9 and 10.

Assets that are both purchased and sold while you are non-resident will not be subject to capital gains tax, even if your period of non-residence lasts for less than five years.

Business Assets

If you are carrying on a 'trade, profession or vocation' in the UK through a branch or agency, any gains that arise from assets connected to that business will be subject to capital gains tax, even if you are non-resident.

If you become non-resident and keep your UK business running you may find that a branch or agency exists.

Thus, while commercial investment property held by non-UK residents is generally exempt from UK capital gains tax, it is important to remember that property used in a trade carried on in the UK by the property's owner (or their agent) may be subject to UK capital gains tax.

Despite this, sales of business assets often qualify for Entrepreneurs Relief (with tax payable at just 10%).

Residential Property from April 2015

Since 6 April 2015, non-UK resident individuals and trusts, as well as many non-UK resident companies, have been subject to capital gains tax when they sell UK residential property.

As a result, almost every person in the world who invests in UK residential property is now exposed to UK capital gains tax.

The good news is that capital gains tax only applies to the part of the gain arising after 5 April 2015. This means that emigration still remains a good tax planning strategy for those with significant capital gains that arose before this date.

Individuals generally pay capital gains tax at two main rates on residential property:

- 18%   basic rate taxpayers
- 28%   higher rate taxpayers

Non-resident individuals who are entitled to the income tax personal allowance need to have total combined UK source income and taxable capital gains of £45,000 in 2017/18 before they start paying tax at 28%.

Those with lower levels of income will pay capital gains tax at 18% on the first part of their capital gains until their basic rate band is used up. Thereafter, any further gains are taxed at 28%.

All individual taxpayers, including non-residents, are entitled to a capital gains tax annual exemption (£11,300 in 2017/18).

Calculating the Taxable Gain

As a non-UK resident the amount of gain subject to tax will generally be limited to the increase in the property's value from 5 April 2015 to the date of sale.

The main, 'default' method for calculating this increase is to base it on the property's actual market value at 5 April 2015. This means it will be necessary to have a proper valuation carried out to determine the property's value as of 5 April 2015. Arguably, the sooner this is done the better.

It is also possible to elect to either:

- Use straight line apportionment

- Pay tax on the gain over their entire period of ownership

Each method produces a different outcome, so it is necessary to find the one which produces the lowest tax bill.

Example

Leonard is non-UK resident. On 5 April 2007 he bought a UK residential property for £250,000. The property was worth £350,000 on 5 April 2015 and he sells it for £400,000 on 5 April 2017.

Under the main default calculation Leonard would be subject to capital gains tax on a gain of £50,000 (£400,000 - £350,000).

If he elects to use straight line apportionment his overall gain is £150,000 (£400,000 - £250,000). He's only subject to capital gains tax for two years out of a total ownership period of 10 years, so this method would give him a chargeable gain of £30,000 (£150,000 x 2/10).

No matter which method Leonard uses, he will be entitled to the 2016/17 annual exemption of £11,100.

Assuming he makes the straight line apportionment election and has no other chargeable gains in the UK in 2016/17, this will leave him with a taxable gain of £18,900 (£30,000 – £11,100).

If we also assume that Leonard has little or no UK-source income in the same 2016/17 tax year then his basic rate band will be available and he only has to pay capital gains tax at 18%.

Leonard's capital gains tax bill will therefore be £3,402 (£18,900 x 18%). He should be able to claim relief for this against any tax liability in the country where he is resident.

Note, although we assumed that Leonard has little or no UK income in this example, if the property is a rental property (or he has other UK rental properties) it is likely he will have taxable rental income.

When combined with his capital gain, the total may exceed the £43,000 higher-rate threshold for 2016/17. In this case he may be subject to the 28% capital gains tax rate on some or all of his capital gain.

Reporting Non-Resident Capital Gains

Non-residents who sell UK residential property after 5 April 2015 are required to report their disposal to HMRC within 30 days.

Those who are in the UK income tax self-assessment system will also need to report their chargeable gains when they submit their tax returns.

Taxpayers who are not in the self-assessment system must pay any capital gains tax due within 30 days of the relevant property disposal.

Non-residents who are already in the UK income tax self-assessment system can currently pay any capital gains tax due by the normal date: 31 January following the end of the tax year.

Note, however, that the Government is proposing to make the

capital gains tax due on all residential property disposals taking place after 5 April 2019 payable within 30 days after the date of disposal. This change will also apply to UK residents.

Relief for Main Residences

Where a property has been used as your main residence (i.e. your principal home) at any time during your period of ownership, you are entitled to an important capital gains tax relief known as principal private residence relief.

Principal private residence relief works on a time apportionment basis and generally exempts that part of your ownership period when the property was your main residence.

It also generally exempts the last 18 months of ownership if, for example, you move out of the property before selling it.

For a non-resident, these periods of exemption will generally only be of any benefit where they fall *after* 5 April 2015: since principal private residence relief can only be claimed on the part of the gain which is actually taxable.

The examples below will help explain these concepts.

Where a property qualifies for principal private residence relief, but has also been rented out at some time during your ownership, it also qualifies for private letting relief.

This relief exempts up to £40,000 of the gain per person, so a couple owning a property jointly may be able to claim up to £80,000 of relief.

However, in the case of non-residents, only letting periods after 5 April 2015 can be counted.

Example

On 5 April 1999, Zari bought a house in the UK for £200,000 and used it as her main residence until she emigrated on 5 April 2013. She kept the property for use during her return visits to the UK.

The house was worth £400,000 on 5 April 2015. Four years later, on 5 April 2019, she sells it for £500,000.

As a non-resident, Zari will be subject to capital gains tax on the gain of £100,000 (£500,000 - £400,000) arising over the 48 month period from April 2015 to April 2019.

Because the property has been her main residence in the past, she is able to claim exemption for her last 18 months of ownership. The exemption amounts to £37,500 (£100,000 x 18/48). She is not entitled to claim private letting relief because she did not rent out the property.

Under the default method for calculating her gain, Zari therefore has a chargeable gain of £62,500 (£100,000 - £37,500).

Zari can also choose from two alternative methods for calculating her gain:

Under the straight line apportionment method, the gain would be £60,000 (£500,000 - £200,000 = £300,000 x 4/20). The number 4/20 represents the four years from April 2015 to 2019 divided by the total number of years she has owned the property.

Zari could then deduct principal private residence relief of £22,500 (£60,000 x 18/48), leaving her with a chargeable gain of £37,500.

By electing to tax the £300,000 gain arising over her whole period of ownership, Zari would be entitled to principal private residence relief for the 14 years she lived in the property and her last 18 months of ownership: a total of 15.5 years, or £232,500 (£300,000 x 15.5/20).

This will leave her with a chargeable gain of £67,500 (£300,000 - £232,500).

Clearly, Zari's best option is to elect for the straight line apportionment method. However this will not always be the case.

In the above example Zari emigrated before April 2015. If you emigrate after this date your principal private residence relief can also include some of the time when you were actually living in the property, not just the final 18 months.

Example

Donna and Simon own a house in London which they bought for £450,000 on 5 April 2011 and was worth £800,000 on 5 April 2015. It remains their main residence until they emigrate on 5 April 2017. They rent the house out for a few years, until they eventually sell it for £1.2m on 5 April 2023 while still non-UK resident.

Under the default method, the gain arising over their relevant ownership period of eight years (2015 to 2023) is £400,000 (£1.2m - £800,000).

The couple are entitled to principal private residence relief for the part of this period that the property was their main residence (April 2015 to April 2017) and for their last eighteen months of ownership. This totals 3.5 years, so their principal private residence relief amounts to £175,000 (£400,000 x 3.5/8).

As the couple rented the property out during their relevant ownership period, they may also claim private letting relief. This is limited to £40,000 each, or £80,000 in total.

Under the default method the couple therefore have a total chargeable gain of £145,000 (£400,000 - £175,000 - £80,000), or £72,500 each.

Under the straight line apportionment method, the total gain arising over their entire 12 year period of ownership is £750,000 (£1.2m - £450,000). The time apportioned gain for the relevant ownership period of eight years is thus £500,000 (£750,000 x 8/12).

As before, Donna and Simon would be entitled to principal private residence relief for 3.5 years out of their relevant ownership period of eight years. This would now amount to £218,750 (£500,000 x 3.5/8). They would also be entitled to private letting relief of £40,000 each, as before. The couple's total chargeable gain would thus now be £201,250 (£500,000 - £218,750 - £80,000), or £100,625 each.

In this example the default method produces the best outcome.

Companies

The new capital gains tax charge also applies to non-resident companies.

More specifically, it applies to "closely held companies" which, generally speaking are companies under the control of five or fewer unconnected individuals.

In broad terms, this means that most non-resident private companies investing in UK residential property will be subject to the new charge.

Companies are generally entitled to use any of the three alternative methods set out above for calculating the chargeable gain (except where the Annual Tax on Enveloped Dwellings applies – see below).

Companies are also entitled to claim indexation relief on their chargeable gains and pay corporation tax, generally 19% from April 2017 (although the charge is still classed as capital gains tax).

Indexation relief is calculated based on the increase in the retail prices index over the relevant period.

Enveloped Dwellings

An additional complication for some non-resident companies is that they are also subject to capital gains tax under the Annual Tax on Enveloped Dwellings rules.

This charge is often known as 'ATED-related capital gains tax' and now generally applies to any residential dwelling in the UK which is not used for 'business purposes' and which is sold for over £500,000.

ATED-related capital gains tax does not apply to individuals or most trusts.

Business use includes renting the property out (to unconnected persons), so most property investment companies will be able to claim exemption from ATED-related capital gains tax, but this charge will apply where property is held for private use.

Where a non-resident company is subject to ATED-related capital gains tax, this charge (which applies at a flat rate of 28% with no indexation relief) takes precedence over the new non-resident capital gains tax charge.

ATED-related capital gains tax only applies to gains that arise after the property falls within the ATED regime.

Some property disposals may be subject to both charges: in this case, the company is not able to elect to use the straight line apportionment method, but may elect to have both charges calculated over the entire period of ownership of the property.

Temporary Absence from Your Home

The principal private residence exemption is generally only available for a period of up to 18 months after you move out of your home.

However, the exemption is available for a period of any length when the taxpayer or their spouse is working in an office or employment whose duties are all performed outside the UK.

This period of temporary absences is only covered if:

- You occupy the property as your main residence both before and after your period of absence

- Neither you nor your spouse have any interest in any other property capable of being treated as your main residence under the principal private residence exemption.

HMRC may, by concession, sometimes accept that you were unable to resume occupation of the property following your absence if you are required to work somewhere else when you return to the UK.

UK Capital Gains Tax Reliefs

It's worth pointing out that UK capital gains tax is 'not always all that bad' and there are plenty of things you can do to reduce it without becoming non-resident.

In fact, in some cases it may be worth disposing of assets *before* you become non-resident because you may end up paying tax at a higher rate in another country.

The top rate of capital gains tax for residential property is 28% but if you are a basic-rate taxpayer the tax rate is just 18%. For most other assets (e.g. commercial property and share investments) the rates have been reduced to 20% and 10% respectively.

Many individuals, including company owners and some retirees, are able to keep their incomes low in years they realize capital gains, allowing them to pay tax at 18% or 10% on some or all of their capital gains.

If you sell or wind up a business there's a good chance you will qualify for Entrepreneurs Relief which means your tax rate will be just 10%.

Thanks to the annual capital gains tax exemption, couples can currently shelter £22,600 of their capital gains from tax.

Most individuals can also shelter most of their stock market profits from tax by investing through ISAs and SIPPs.

When you sell a property that was your main residence you can benefit from the principal private residence exemption. This exemption covers the period during which the property was your main residence plus the last 18 months of ownership.

Additionally, any property that qualifies as your main residence at any time during your period of ownership, and which you rent out, will also qualify for up to £40,000 of private letting relief.

There are lots of other things a UK resident can do to avoid capital gains tax and these are covered in other Taxcafe guides including *How to Save Property Tax* and *Salary versus Dividends*.

Chapter 23

Overseas Capital Gains Tax

No Capital Gains Tax

The following countries generally do not tax capital gains

- Argentina
- Aruba
- Bahamas
- Bahrain
- Bermuda
- Brunei
- Cayman Islands
- Costa Rica
- Curacao
- Gibraltar
- Guernsey
- Hong Kong
- Isle of Man
- Jamaica
- Jersey
- Jordan
- Kuwait
- Macau
- Mauritius
- New Zealand
- Papua New Guinea
- Qatar
- Singapore
- Sint Maarten
- Swaziland
- Switzerland
- United Arab Emirates

In the above table there are some exceptions, however.

In Aruba capital gains from selling business assets are taxed at a rate of up to 58.95%. Capital gains from selling shares in a company are also taxed if you own 25% or more of the company.

Gains derived by Argentine resident individuals from the sale of shares, bonds and other securities not listed on a stock exchange or publicly traded are subject to income tax at a rate of 15%.

In Costa Rica capital gains are generally exempt but are taxable if they arise from business activities in certain cases.

In Curacao, capital gains are generally exempt. However, business assets are taxed at up to 46.5%. Substantial interests in companies are taxed at 19.5%.

In New Zealand, capital gains are generally exempt. However, gains from real or personal property may be subject to income tax if your business consists of dealing in that type of property or if your intention at the time of buying was to sell at a later date. Gains from the sale of residential property (other than your main home) that is sold within two years are also taxable.

In Papua New Guinea, capital gains are generally exempt. However, if the sale is part of a profit-making scheme or is part of your ordinary business it may be subject to tax.

In Qatar, capital gains are generally tax free but may be taxable if the assets are part of a 'taxable activity'.

In Singapore, capital gains may be taxed if they are related to the carrying on of a trade.

In Sint Maarten, profits from selling business assets or liquidating a company may be subject to income tax at rates of up to 47.5%.

In Switzerland private capital gains are generally not taxed at the federal level but the cantons levy tax on immoveable assets. Business assets are usually taxed by both the federal government and the cantons.

Popular Destinations

Most people do not emigrate to tax havens or countries with low tax rates. Most popular destinations tax capital gains, although gains from the sale of principal residences are generally exempt in most countries.

Australia

There is no separate capital gains tax. Capital gains are included in income and taxed at rates of up to 45%. For assets held for more than one year there is a capital gains discount and tax is payable on half the capital gain, which means the top rate is 22.5%.

Capital gains from the sale of your principal residence are generally exempt.

Temporary residents cannot benefit from the capital gains tax discount. Temporary residents are those with temporary visas who are not married to Australian citizens or permanent residents.

Temporary residents only have to pay tax on their Taxable Australian Property (typically Australian real estate). Their overseas capital gains, for example from UK assets, are exempt.

United States

Generally speaking assets held for more than 12 months (long-term gains) are taxed at the following rates:

Individuals in the 10% or 15% tax bracket	0%
Individuals in the 39.6% tax bracket	20%
Individuals in other tax brackets	15%

Short-term capital gains (assets held for less than 12 months) are taxed as ordinary income.

Spain

At present Spain has an additional levy on capital gains made by tax residents. The rates are:

€0 - €5,999	19%
€6,000 - €49,999	21%
€50,000 or more	23%

Capital gains tax may not be payable when you sell your main residence, as long as you've lived in it for three years and reinvest all the money in a new main residence somewhere in the EU.

Over-65s do not have to reinvest as long as the property has been their main residence for more than three years.

Spanish residents pay capital gains tax on all other property sales worldwide.

Canada

50% of capital gains are included in income. Thus the top effective federal rate is 16.5%. When combined with taxes levied by the provinces (e.g. British Columbia, Ontario etc) the top tax rates vary from 22.25% to 27%.

Ireland

Capital gains are generally taxed at 33% but non-domiciled individuals are not taxed on their non-Irish capital gains unless the proceeds are remitted to Ireland.

France

Capital gains from movable assets such as shares are taxed as regular income at rates of up to 45% plus social security charges of roughly 15.5%. The tax rate is reduced for assets held for more than two years.

There is also a special tax regime for expatriates seconded to France (Article 155B). There is also a 50% tax exemption with respect to foreign source dividends interest and capital gains (from the sale of securities) for a period of five years, although social surtaxes of 15.5% remain payable.

Capital gains from immovable property are generally taxed at a flat rate of 19% plus social security charges of 15.5% producing a combined tax rate of 34.5%. After five years of ownership the taxable gain is reduced each year. Once the property is held for 30 years there is no taxable gain.

A supplementary tax is also payable on gains in excess of €50,000 at rates of between 2% and 6%, depending on the size of the gain.

South Africa

40% of capital gains are included in income and taxed. Therefore, with a top income tax rate of 41%, the effective capital gains tax rate for someone taxed at the highest rate is 16.4%. There is also a small exemption of R40,000.

Part 4

Tax Saving Tactics for Non Doms

Chapter 24

How Domicile Affects Your Tax

If you are UK resident but not domiciled in the UK there are special rules that apply to your overseas income and capital gains.

Essentially you may be able to choose to be taxed according to the *remittance basis*. This means that UK tax will only be payable on your *overseas* income and capital gains if and when the money is brought into the UK.

You will still, however, have to pay UK tax on your UK income and capital gains, just like anyone else.

If you do not have any foreign income or capital gains your domicile status generally has no bearing on the amount of income tax or capital gains tax you pay. If all your income and gains come from UK sources you will pay UK tax just like anyone else.

As we shall see, making a claim to pay tax under the remittance basis can be very costly. Not only will you lose your personal allowance and annual capital gains tax exemption, you may also have to pay the £30,000 or £60,000 remittance basis charge if you've been living in the UK for a certain length of time.

Having said this, there are some useful exemptions that allow non-domiciled individuals who cannot afford to pay the remittance basis charge to benefit from their special tax status. These are outlined in the pages that follow.

As an alternative to the remittance basis, you can accept the default position and allow yourself to be taxed on the *arising basis*. Under the arising basis, tax is payable on all your UK and overseas income and capital gains as they arise. This is how most UK residents are taxed.

When it comes to inheritance tax your residence status generally isn't important. It's your domicile that matters and the location of your assets. If you are UK domiciled you will be subject to UK inheritance tax on your worldwide assets, even if you are non-resident.

If you are treated as non-domiciled, your UK assets will still be subject to inheritance tax. However, your overseas assets are "excluded property" and are not subject to inheritance tax.

Becoming Deemed UK Domiciled

From 6 April 2017, once you have been UK resident for 15 out of the last 20 tax years, you will become "deemed UK domiciled" for income tax, capital gains tax and inheritance tax purposes.

Thus many non-doms who are long-term UK residents will immediately become deemed UK domiciled for tax purposes on 6 April 2017.

Children who are born and brought up in the UK, but are not domiciled here, will become deemed UK domiciled for tax purposes before reaching adulthood.

Becoming deemed UK domiciled means you can no longer use the remittance basis for your overseas income and capital gains. Just like most other UK residents, all of your income and capital gains will be taxed as they arise.

Unremitted income and capital gains from previous tax years will still be taxed on the remittance basis, i.e. they will be tax-free if kept outside the UK and taxed if remitted to the UK.

As far as inheritance tax is concerned, once you become deemed UK domiciled both your UK and overseas assets will be subject to UK inheritance tax.

As part of a recent package of tax reforms affecting non doms, the Government is also clamping down heavily on individuals who were born with a UK domicile and then emigrate and acquire a domicile elsewhere before returning to the UK.

We will take a closer look at deemed UK domicile in Chapter 27.

Please note, many of the changes discussed in the chapters that follow form part of the 2017 Finance Bill. This legislation has not been passed yet and it is possible that further changes or amendments will be made.

Chapter 25

Where Are You Domiciled?

In this chapter we will ignore the fact that you can become deemed UK domiciled for tax purposes, typically once you've been UK resident for 15 out of the last 20 tax years. Instead we'll examine how your true underlying domicile status is determined.

Generally speaking your domicile is the country you consider to be your permanent home. This is not necessarily the country where you were born or the country where you are living at present.

Whereas it is relatively easy to change your residence status for tax purposes, your domicile is much harder to change.

Domicile is largely a question of intention. If you are not UK domiciled it should be difficult for HMRC to prove that you have become UK domiciled, unless you have stated that it is your intention to live in the UK permanently (for example, on an HMRC form).

You could live in the UK for 50 years and still be non-UK domiciled if you still intend to eventually return to your homeland.

By the same token, if you're currently UK domiciled and emigrate, you may find it difficult to convince the taxman that you have lost your UK domicile and acquired a new one somewhere else.

Although the UK's tax laws refer to UK domicile, technically speaking you cannot actually have UK domicile. You are either domiciled in England and Wales, Scotland or Northern Ireland.

There are three types of domicile:

- Domicile of origin
- Domicile of choice
- Domicile of dependence

Domicile of Origin

Every person acquires a domicile of origin from one of their parents when they are born. Your domicile or origin is not necessarily the country where you are born.

If your parents were married when you were born, you acquire your father's domicile. If your parents were not married when you were born, you acquire your mother's domicile.

For example, a child born in wedlock in France to a UK domiciled father will have a UK domicile of origin. A child born in wedlock in the UK to an Australian domiciled father will have an Australian domicile of origin.

Thus an individual's domicile of origin could be a country they have never visited. Although a domicile of origin can be replaced if you acquire a new domicile of choice, it remains in the background and may be resurrected at a later date, for example if you lose your domicile of choice later on.

Example

Winston has a UK domicile of origin. He emigrates to New Zealand and acquires a New Zealand domicile of choice because it is his intention to live there permanently. However, after 10 years he decides it's time for a change and moves to Hong Kong. He no longer intends to live in New Zealand permanently but he also isn't sure that he wants to live in Hong Kong permanently either. As a result his UK domicile of origin is resurrected.

In Scotland the Family Law (Scotland) Act 2006 abolished the status of illegitimacy and so the domicile status of children born in and out of wedlock is determined in the same manner.

Children under 16 are domiciled in the same country as their parents if both parents are domiciled in the same country and the child has a home with one or both of them. Where the parents have different domicile, children under 16 are domiciled in the country with which the child has the closest connection.

Domicile of Dependency

This type of domicile mainly applies to children under the age of 16 whose parents change their domicile. If the relevant parent's domicile status changes, the parent's new domicile of choice becomes the child's domicile of dependency.

At age 16 the domicile of dependency continues but is reclassified as a domicile of choice.

Example

Dave and Kirsty are married and both are UK domiciled. Their son Matthew, aged 10, also has a UK domicile of origin. The family emigrate to France and acquire a French domicile of choice. Matthew acquires a French domicile of dependency from his father. When Matthew turns 16 his French domicile of dependency will become a French domicile of choice.

If unmarried parents subsequently marry, a child born outside marriage retains the domicile of origin he acquired from his mother but this is replaced by a domicile of dependence that he acquires from his father.

If the parents of a child born in wedlock separate and the child lives with the mother, then the child's domicile of dependence is that of the mother.

Married Women

For marriages before 1 January 1974 women automatically acquired a domicile of dependence from their husbands. This rule was abolished but women married before 1 January 1974 still keep the domicile they acquired from their husbands, albeit reclassified as a domicile of choice.

Since 1974 women have not acquired a domicile of dependence from their husbands – their domicile status is determined according to the normal rules.

Under the terms of the UK/US double tax agreement, female US citizens who married UK domiciled men before 1 January 1974 do not acquire their husbands' domicile automatically for income tax and capital gains tax purposes. Their domicile is determined under the normal rules.

Domicile of Choice

In most cases you keep your domicile of origin for the rest of your life. However, a new domicile of choice can be acquired voluntarily if you reside in another country and can prove that you intend to live there permanently or indefinitely.

According to HMRC: *"For domicile purposes, particularly where your domicile changes from one in the UK, you may need to provide strong evidence that you intend to live in another country permanently or indefinitely. The following factors will be relevant, although this list is not exhaustive:*

- *your intentions*
- *your permanent residence*
- *your business interests*
- *your social and family interests*
- *your ownership of property*
- *the form of any will you have made*

You should therefore maintain records that will allow you to satisfy HMRC of the centre of your interests in the above areas, should we enquire into your domicile status."

The term domicile of *choice* is misleading because it is possible to acquire a domicile of choice even if you don't want it. For example, a non-UK domiciled individual who lives in the UK may acquire a UK domicile of choice unintentionally if it can be shown that he intends to live in the country permanently. The individual may not want to be UK domiciled but the evidence may point in that direction.

In practice, it may be difficult to prove that you have acquired a new domicile of choice because it may be difficult to prove that your intention is to live permanently or indefinitely in a particular country. The burden of proof lies with the person who alleges that a change has taken place – in some cases the taxpayer himself, in other cases the taxman.

This burden of proof can be both good news and bad news. For example, it may be bad news if you are UK domiciled and emigrate and want to prove that you have lost your UK domicile for inheritance tax purposes.

However, it may be good news if you are foreign domiciled and live in the UK for many years but do not want to be treated as UK domiciled. It may be very difficult for HMRC to prove that you have acquired a new domicile of choice in the UK, especially if you can show that it is your intention to return to your country of origin one day.

Where HMRC may find it easier to challenge your domicile status is after you have died and inheritance tax is at stake. At this stage you can no longer state your intentions and HMRC may be able to show that the evidence points to you being UK domiciled.

The length of time you spend in a country is indicative but not conclusive in proving that you have acquired a new domicile. In one court case it was held that an individual who had lived in the UK for more than 40 years and had a Canadian domicile of origin had not acquired a UK domicile of choice because he always intended to return to Canada after his wife died.

Of course, someone who has lived in the UK this long would now be deemed UK domiciled for tax purposes. Generally speaking, HMRC no longer has to prove that long-term UK residents have acquired a new domicile of choice in the UK to tax them.

Nevertheless, it's important to point out that becoming deemed UK domiciled is not the same as a change of domicile under general law. For example, as we shall see in Chapter 27, an individual who is deemed UK domiciled, can become non-UK domiciled again for tax purposes after leaving the country.

If you emigrate and acquire a new nationality and passport, this will not provide conclusive evidence that your domicile has changed. To acquire a new domicile of choice you have to demonstrate an intention to make another country your permanent home and follow this up with action.

There is no set procedure for establishing a new domicile of choice by emigrating. Like many things in the tax world, each individual case will be examined on its own particular merits. However, many tax advisors recommend doing things like:

- Buying a grave plot in your new country
- Establishing citizenship/nationality in your new country
- Writing a will in your new country
- Buying a home in your new country and selling your UK home
- Closing UK bank accounts
- Getting a job or starting a new business in your new country
- Resigning from UK clubs and associations

Genuine statements you make to friends and family (both verbally and in writing) about your intention to live in any particular country could provide crucial evidence in determining your domicile status and may be more credible than statements made on official forms or in formal documents such as your will which may be treated with suspicion.

If you spend time in more than one country, determining your domicile status may become more difficult. It will be necessary to determine which one is the centre of your interests, in other words your chief or principal residence and that you have an intention to live there permanently or indefinitely.

In the very high-profile Gaines-Cooper case, Robert Gaines-Cooper had a UK domicile of origin but contended that he had acquired a domicile of choice in the Seychelles.

Despite building up significant links in the Seychelles (he bought a house there and stated in his will that he was Seychelles domiciled and wanted his ashes scattered there), the court decided that he had not acquired a Seychelles domicile of choice. He also had strong UK connections, including a number of homes in the UK, an English will, British citizenship (he did not apply for citizenship in the Seychelles) and lots of past and current business and family connections to Berkshire and Oxfordshire.

Once a domicile of choice is abandoned the domicile of origin reasserts itself until another domicile of choice is acquired.

In *Henwood v Barlow Clowes International*, Henwood was originally domiciled in England and Wales but acquired a domicile of choice in the Isle of Man. He then moved to Mauritius on a trial basis.

He admitted that he no longer intended to live in the Isle of Man permanently or indefinitely and had thus abandoned his domicile of choice in the Isle of Man.

The court stated that it would be impossible to have immediately acquired a new domicile of choice in Mauritius because he was living there on a trial basis. Thus his UK domicile of origin was revived.

Where Are You Domiciled?

As can be seen from the above discussion, domicile is a somewhat 'airy-fairy' concept. Many individuals will not know for certain whether they are, in fact, non-UK domiciled or whether the taxman will ultimately challenge them.

HMRC does not provide formal domicile rulings. That's up to the courts to do and there have been numerous, presumably expensive, battles between HMRC and taxpayers over the years.

HMRC may challenge your claim to be non-domiciled if you have already taken action (for example, placed assets into a trust to avoid inheritance tax) and there is a considerable amount of tax at stake.

According to HMRC, *"We do not normally challenge any person who says they have a UK domicile. If you say you have a non-UK domicile, we might want to check whether or not that is correct, particularly if you were born in the UK.*

"By its very nature, a check aimed at establishing your domicile will be an in-depth examination of:

- *your background*
- *lifestyle*
- *your intentions over the course of your lifetime.*

"Any check of this sort will extend to areas of your life, and that of your family, that you might not normally think are relevant to your UK tax affairs. We will need to ask these questions and sometimes ask you to provide us with evidence about these areas of your life, as part of our check. This may involve meeting with you in person."

If you wish to take tax planning action based on the assumption that you are non-UK domiciled, but you are not 100% certain that you are non-UK domiciled, it is vital to obtain professional advice as to your domicile status before proceeding.

Chapter 26

The Remittance Basis: Introduction

Normally UK residents pay tax on their worldwide income and capital gains. However, non-domiciled individuals who are not deemed UK domiciled (see Chapter 27) can use the remittance basis to avoid paying income tax and capital gains tax on their *overseas* investments.

Remittance basis users generally don't have to pay UK tax on their unremitted income and capital gains (i.e. income or capital gains that are kept overseas). They do, however, have to pay tax on their UK income and capital gains, just like everyone else.

Up until recently UK residents who were not 'ordinarily resident' could also use the remittance basis. However, the concept of ordinary residence has now been abolished.

Remittance basis users do not necessarily avoid UK tax permanently. If you've used the remittance basis in a previous tax year and bring some of the income or capital gains into the UK at a later date, the remittance may then be subject to UK tax.

2008 Changes

In 2008 there were significant changes to the way the remittance basis operates. Nowadays, non-domiciled individuals must make a choice each year between being taxed on the remittance basis or the arising basis.

If you wish to be taxed on the remittance basis you have to actively elect to be taxed this way when you complete your tax return. Making the election comes at a price which includes losing your income tax personal allowance and annual capital gains tax exemption and possibly paying the remittance charge.

This charge is £30,000 if you have been resident for 7 of the past 9 tax years and rises to £60,000 when you have been resident for 12 of the past 14 tax years. Once you've been UK resident for 15 out of the last 20 tax years, you will become "deemed UK domiciled" and can no longer claim the remittance basis.

If you don't elect to be taxed under the remittance basis, you will automatically be taxed under the arising basis. The arising basis is the way most UK residents are taxed and means you will pay tax on your worldwide income and capital gains, regardless of whether you keep your foreign income and capital gains offshore or bring the money into the UK.

What Is a Remittance?

Generally speaking, if you are taxed on the remittance basis you only pay tax when you bring your overseas income or capital gains into the UK.

HMRC interprets the term 'remittance' widely. For example, you may end up paying tax on overseas income or gains given to close family members and other 'relevant persons' in the UK.

Relevant persons include:

- The non-domiciled individual
- His spouse, civil partner or unmarried partner
- Children and grandchildren under 18
- Close companies in which the individual or another relevant person is a participator
- Trustees where a relevant person is a beneficiary of the trust

If you buy assets with your overseas income or gains and bring them into the UK, this can also trigger a taxable remittance. For example, if you buy an expensive painting overseas and bring it into the UK this may be treated as a taxable remittance.

Credit Cards & Debit Cards

A remittance may also be triggered if you use your overseas income or capital gains to satisfy a 'relevant debt'. For example, if you use a UK credit card to pay for goods or services (either in the UK or overseas) and then settle the credit card bill using overseas income or gains, the payment will be a taxable remittance.

If you use an overseas credit card in the UK this will also create a 'relevant debt'. Thus, if you use your untaxed foreign income or gains to pay the credit card company, this will trigger a taxable remittance.

However, if you use an overseas credit card overseas, you can use your overseas income and capital gains to settle the bill without creating a taxable remittance.

If you buy things with a debit card issued by an overseas financial institution the payment will be treated in exactly the same way as a cash transaction. This means that if you pay for things in the UK a taxable remittance is made to the extent of the amount of any overseas income or gains in the bank account. Likewise any cash withdrawals from shops or ATM machines in the UK are taxable cash remittances.

However, any payment that relates to overseas goods or services would not usually be classed as a taxable remittance.

Clean Capital

As part of the recent package of tax reforms, non-domiciled individuals have been given a one off opportunity to segregate their so-called "mixed funds" so that more tax-efficient remittances can be made to the UK in the future.

Before we explain this concession it's first important to explain the concept of "clean capital". If you are UK resident and non-domiciled, you can bring clean capital into the UK without paying tax. Clean capital is typically overseas income and capital gains that were earned before you became UK resident. It can also include gifts and inherited money.

Once you become UK resident, the overseas income and capital gains you earn from that point on will be subject to UK tax as they arise but you can elect to be taxed under the remittance basis which means tax will only be payable if the money is brought into the UK. This election does, however, come at a price and once you've been UK resident for 15 out of the last 20 tax years you will be deemed UK domiciled and will pay tax on all your worldwide income and gains as they arise (see Chapter 27).

However, it is possible to structure your affairs so that only clean capital is remitted. To do this it is essential that the clean capital is ring fenced, i.e. kept separate from the income and capital gains that arise after you become UK resident.

If your clean capital gets mixed with your post-arrival income and capital gains this creates a "mixed fund". Remittances from a mixed fund are subject to special ordering rules which typically tax you in the least favourable way. Any income that is in the mixed fund is treated as remitted first, followed by capital gains and finally your clean capital.

This can make it difficult for non-domiciled individuals to get their hands on clean capital without paying tax. Once a mixed fund has been created it is usually not possible to "unmix" it.

Keeping your clean capital properly segregated can be extremely difficult in practice, for example making sure income or capital gains that arise after you become UK resident are not paid into a clean capital account before being transferred into a separate bank account.

From 6 April 2017 non doms are being given a two year window (i.e. until 5 April 2019) to separate their mixed funds into separate accounts for income, capital gains and tax-free capital.

This will allow them to bring their clean capital into the UK tax free. Income and capital gains that are remitted will be taxed accordingly.

The concession only applies to mixed funds deposited in bank accounts and similar accounts.

It's available to all non doms who have claimed the remittance basis at some point before 2017/18 (except those born in the UK with a UK domicile of origin).

In the March 2017 Budget it was announced that the rules will be extended to income, gains and capital held in mixed funds from years before 2007/08, as well as those from subsequent years.

Chapter 27

Deemed UK Domiciled: The New Rules

From 6 April 2017, once you've been UK resident for 15 out of the last 20 tax years, you will become "deemed UK domiciled" for income tax, capital gains tax and inheritance tax purposes.

Becoming deemed UK domiciled means you can no longer use the remittance basis for your overseas income and capital gains. Just like most other UK residents, all of your income and capital gains will be taxed on the arising basis, i.e. each year as they arise.

Unremitted income and capital gains from previous tax years will still be taxed on the remittance basis, i.e. they will be tax-free if kept outside the UK and taxed if remitted to the UK.

As far as inheritance tax is concerned, once you are deemed UK domiciled both your UK and overseas assets will be subject to UK inheritance tax (non doms are normally not subject to inheritance tax on their overseas assets).

If you become deemed domiciled and later leave the UK, you can come back and enjoy another non-domiciled period of 15 years.

However, to become non-domiciled again for tax purposes you have to stay out of the UK for at least six tax years. It will also be necessary to remain non-UK domiciled under normal law.

For inheritance tax purposes, if a deemed domiciled person ceases to be UK resident they will lose their deemed UK domiciled status after being non-resident for three tax years, providing they do not return to the UK within six years. So if you return in years four, five or six, the 15/20 years rule will apply for all tax purposes.

Some tax commentators believe that non-domiciled individuals who return to the UK after six years may face increased scrutiny from HMRC as to whether they are genuinely still non-UK domiciled or whether they have decided to make the UK their permanent home.

For the 15/20 years test, any tax year which is a split year under the Statutory Residence Test will be counted as a year in which the individual is UK resident. Those who wish to avoid becoming deemed UK domiciled may therefore need to consider emigrating before the start of their 15th year of residence.

When working out your residence status for any particular tax year in order to decide whether you're deemed UK domiciled, you have to use the rules that were in place in the year in question.

Thus from 2013/14 onwards you use the Statutory Residence Test to decide your residence status. For earlier tax years you have to rely on the old rules contained in HMRC's guidance derived from case law (see Chapter 1).

Born in UK with UK Domicile of Origin

If an individual is born in the UK with a UK domicile of origin and then emigrates, it's possible they will acquire a domicile of choice in another country.

However, if such an individual returns and becomes UK resident again, he or she will become deemed UK domiciled again for income tax and capital gains tax purposes for as long as they are UK resident. This rule applies from 6 April 2017.

By concession there will be a grace period before overseas assets are subject to inheritance tax. This is designed to help those returning to the UK for a short time only.

The individual will only be subject to inheritance tax if they were also UK resident in one of the previous two tax years as well as the tax year in question.

Offshore trusts that the individual or his close family can benefit from will lose their special tax status, which means tax may be payable on the trust's income and capital gains as they arise and the trust's assets may form part of the individual's estate for inheritance tax purposes.

Capital Gain Tax Rebasing

If you become deemed UK domiciled and then sell overseas assets (or UK assets for that matter) you will be subject to capital gains tax on the arising basis, just like most people who live in this country.

However, if you become deemed UK domiciled on 6 April 2017 (but no later), any capital gains that arose on your overseas assets *before* 6 April 2017 will not be subject to UK capital gains tax. Your overseas assets will be rebased to their value on 5 April 2017.

Any increase in the value of your assets after this date will be subject to capital gains tax in the normal way.

It may be possible to bring the tax-free component of any gain, which arose before 6 April 2017, into the UK with no further tax charge, if properly segregated.

Where the asset was originally bought with "clean capital", the entire proceeds from the disposal can be brought to the UK without triggering a remittance.

However, where the asset was purchased using foreign income or capital gains, some of the sale proceeds will still relate to that earlier income and gains and will be taxed if remitted to the UK.

Rebasing is automatic but can be disapplied, for example if the asset's value on 5 April 2017 is less than the purchase price.

There are a number of conditions if you want to benefit from rebasing, for example:

- Rebasing is only possible if you have paid the remittance basis charge at some point in the past (i.e. for any tax year up to and including 2016/17). It's not good enough to merely have claimed the remittance basis. At the time of writing, there was some uncertainty as to whether this requirement to have paid the remittance charge would be retained in the final legislation.

- Assets held in offshore trusts and companies will not benefit from rebasing, only assets held *personally*.

- UK assets don't qualify so the assets must not have been located in the UK between 16 March 2016 and 5 April 2017.

- Rebasing is not available to those were born in the UK with a UK domicile of origin.

- Those who become deemed-domiciled in years after 6 April 2017 will not be able to rebase their overseas assets.

Chapter 28

The Tax Benefits of Offshore Trusts

Trust Basics

A trust is a structure into which you can pass ownership and control of your assets. The person who puts his assets into a trust is called the settlor.

He or she may have many different reasons for setting up a trust, for example to save tax, protect assets from creditors or to safeguard wealth for future generations (for example, where parents are reluctant to give their children significant sums of money for fear that it will be squandered by them or their spouses).

The trust's assets are managed by trustees (for example, a firm of solicitors or accountants and maybe the settlor and his spouse) on behalf of the beneficiaries (typically family members).

Tax advisors often use the term "settlement" to describe the act of creating a trust or the trust itself.

No formalities are required to set up a trust, although in most cases there is a formal trust deed which provides evidence that a trust has been created, who the beneficiaries are and sets out how the trust is to be run (for example, how trustees are to be appointed and what their powers are).

Offshore Trusts

Just like individuals and companies, trusts can be UK resident or non-resident. Non-resident trusts (also known as offshore trusts) are often set up in tax havens or low-tax jurisdictions such as the Channel Islands.

A trust's residence status depends on the residence status of the trustees:

- If all the trustees are UK resident, the trust is UK resident

- If all the trustees are non-resident, the trust is non-resident

- If there is a mixture of UK resident and non-resident trustees the trust will only be non-resident if the settlor was non-resident and non-domiciled when the trust was set up or when funds are added

It's important to make sure that appointing a trustee doesn't inadvertently make the trust UK resident. If a UK resident wants to set up an offshore trust he cannot also be a trustee.

Note that a non-resident trustee is deemed to be UK resident if he is carrying on a business in the UK through a "branch, agency or permanent establishment". Therefore great care needs to be taken if there is an offshore trustee with many UK connections.

Tax Treatment

The tax treatment of non-resident trusts is changing with effect from 6 April 2017.

The good news is that if a non-domiciled individual sets up an offshore trust *before* becoming deemed UK domiciled under the 15/20 years rule, the trust's overseas income and capital gains will NOT be taxed in the hands of the settlor as they arise.

Offshore trusts will, therefore, continue to be attractive vehicles for rolling up family wealth tax free.

UK source income will, however, be taxed in the hands of the settlor as it arises.

There is, however, a condition to enjoy this tax protection: no new funds or property can be added to the trust after the settlor becomes deemed UK domiciled (although there are some exceptions, for example where payments are made to cover the trust's admin costs or tax bill, where the expenses exceed the trust's income for the year).

The settlor must also remain non-UK domiciled under general law and must not be a formerly UK domiciled resident (i.e. someone who was born in the UK with a UK domicile of origin but acquires an overseas domicile of choice before returning to the UK).

If new property is added to the trust after the settlor becomes deemed UK domiciled, all income and capital gains from that point onwards will be taxed in the hands of the settlor as they arise (in other words, the trust will become "transparent" for tax purposes). This is the same anti-avoidance rule that generally applies to those setting up trusts who are UK resident and UK domiciled.

Although offshore trusts can still be used to roll up wealth tax free, tax may still be payable when money is taken out of the trust and new rules are being introduced to prevent tax avoidance.

Tax on Trust Payments

At the time of writing the new legislation dealing with some of the tax treatment of payments from non-resident trusts had not been finalized, so the following is subject to change.

A trust will not lose its "tax-free status" if payments are made to the settlor and his family. However, the person who receives the payment may have to pay income tax or capital gains tax.

In some cases the settlor will have to pay tax on benefits received by close family members where those family members are not subject to UK tax (for example where the recipient is non-UK resident or a UK resident non dom who claims the remittance basis). The settlor can then recover the tax paid from the beneficiary or from the trustees.

If the recipient is a UK resident and pays tax on the arising basis then the recipient will pay the tax.

Close family includes spouses, unmarried couples who live together as a married couple and minor children.

It would appear that this rule will apply to all settlors who are UK resident but non-domiciled and not just those who are deemed UK domiciled.

Where the settlor claims the remittance basis and the payment to him or the close family member has not been remitted, there will be no tax charge initially, although tax will be payable if the payment is brought into the UK at a later date.

Where the settlor is UK resident and deemed UK domiciled under the 15/20 years rule, the remittance basis will not be available which means tax will be payable even if the payment is made outside the UK. Similarly, if the payment is received by a close family member who is non-UK resident the settlor will be subject to tax.

"Washing Out" Trust Capital Gains

It used to be possible to pay out a trust's stockpiled capital gains tax free to a non-resident beneficiary. This reduced the taxable gains of the trust on which UK beneficiaries would be taxed.

From 6 April 2017, distributions to non-residents will no longer "wash out" the stockpiled gains inside the trust. As a result, the trust's capital gains will continue to be matched against payments to UK resident beneficiaries or non-residents who are close family members of the UK resident settlor.

These rules will apply to all non-resident trusts regardless of the domicile status of the settlor (i.e. it doesn't matter whether the settlor is non-domiciled, UK domiciled or deemed UK domiciled).

Rules to Prevent Recycling

Under the previous tax regime it was possible in certain circumstances for a non-resident trust to make a tax-free payment to a beneficiary (for example, if the beneficiary was non-resident or non-domiciled and used the remittance basis). The funds could then be gifted to someone else, for example somebody who would have been taxed if the payment came directly from the trust.

A new anti-avoidance rule is being introduced to prevent funds being recycled in this manner, for example where the settlor would not be liable to pay income tax or capital gains tax because the distribution is made to a non-resident who is also not a close relative (e.g. an adult child).

If a distribution is made to a beneficiary who is non-resident or uses the remittance basis and that person then makes a gift to a UK resident (not just the settlor), the gift will be treated as a trust distribution to that UK resident and taxed.

This will generally only happen if the gift takes place within three years of the trust distribution, although the time period will be longer when "arrangements" are in place to recycle money.

Benefits in Kind

Where an interest-free loan is received from an offshore trust the annual taxable benefit is found by multiplying the amount of the loan by the official rate of interest (currently 3%), less the amount of interest actually paid to the trust (not simply rolled up).

Where a settlor has lent money to an offshore trust and this is repaid after 5 April 2017, a charge to income tax may arise on the repayment of that loan if the trust has accumulated income.

Chapter 29

Three Important Concessions for Non Doms

Income/Capital Gains Under £2,000

There is a very important concession for non-domiciled individuals with small amounts of unremitted income and capital gains. If your unremitted income and gains for the year are less than £2,000, the money can be kept tax free overseas and you will not lose your personal allowance or capital gains tax exemption and will not have to pay the remittance basis charge.

This exemption will remain available even after an individual becomes deemed UK domiciled for tax purposes.

If you are a higher-rate taxpayer, this concession could save you £799.60 in tax every year:

$$£1,999 \times 40\% \text{ tax} = £799.60$$

For couples who are both non-domiciled the total potential tax saving is £1,599:

$$£1,999 \times 2 \times 40\% = £1,599$$

The figure £1,999 is used because your unremitted overseas income and gains must be *less than* £2,000. If you have £2,000 or more you do not qualify.

The concession is more generous than it appears. A non-domiciled individual who earns, say, 3% income can effectively keep around £65,000 offshore and out of the UK taxman's clutches. Couples who are both non-domiciled can keep almost £130,000 offshore and not worry about UK tax on the income.

You can get your hands on these tax savings by simply spending the money when you travel abroad.

It's important to point out that you may be able to benefit from this concession even if your total overseas income exceeds £1,999. What matters is how much *unremitted* overseas income you have, not your total overseas income. As long as you remit the rest of your income and gains to the UK and pay tax you will still qualify. For example, if you earn £10,000 overseas income during the year, you can remit £8,001 to the UK and pay tax on it and keep £1,999 offshore and tax free.

Your unremitted foreign income is calculated by deducting the foreign income you have remitted during the tax year from your total foreign income. The balance is your unremitted foreign income. This is converted into pounds sterling at the exchange rate on the last day of the tax year.

For capital gains you use the exchange rate at the date the asset is sold. For any expenses that are allowed as a deduction you use the prevailing exchange rate on the date the expenses were incurred.

If your unremitted foreign income and gains are less than £2,000 you will be automatically taxed on the remittance basis without necessarily having to complete a tax return. If you complete a tax return anyway you would complete the *Residence, Remittance Basis* supplementary pages which contain a tick box for those with less than £2,000 of unremitted income and capital gains.

If your unremitted foreign income and gains are £2,000 or more, you'll have to make a claim to be taxed on the remittance basis. You can only do this if you are not deemed UK domiciled.

You will lose your personal allowance and annual CGT exemption and may have to pay the £30,000 or £60,000 remittance basis charge.

If you do not make a claim to be taxed on the remittance basis or are deemed UK domiciled you will be taxed under the arising basis on your worldwide income and gains.

Finally, those with small amounts of overseas investment income may not have to pay any UK tax under the arising basis thanks to the savings and dividend allowances. All UK resident individuals can currently enjoy £5,000 of tax-free dividend income (£2,000 from April 2018) and up to £1,000 of tax-free interest each year (£500 for higher-rate taxpayers, £0 for additional-rate taxpayers). These allowances can be used for both UK and overseas income.

Non Doms with Little or No UK Income

Non-domiciled individuals can also benefit from the remittance basis without preparing a tax return and making a formal claim if:

- They have no UK income or capital gains for the tax year in question, except taxed UK investment income of under £100, and

- They make no remittances of overseas income and gains during the tax year, and

- They have been UK resident in fewer than 7 out of the previous 9 tax years or they are under 18 throughout the tax year.

Individuals who meet these criteria do not have to complete a tax return to claim the remittance basis. They do not lose their personal allowance or annual capital gains tax exemption.

A non-domiciled spouse with no UK income in their own name is one example of the type of person who could benefit from the remittance basis in this way without having to make a claim and complete a tax return.

Small Amounts of Foreign Employment Income

There is also an exemption for non-domiciled individuals with small amounts of overseas employment income. To qualify all of the following conditions must be met for the tax year in question:

- You must be employed in the UK
- You must be a basic-rate taxpayer (based on your worldwide income and capital gains)
- Your foreign employment income must be less than £10,000
- Your overseas bank interest must be less than £100
- All your overseas employment income and interest must be subject to tax overseas
- You have no other overseas income or gains
- You do not have to complete a tax return for any other reason

If you meet all of these conditions your foreign income is effectively free from UK tax (even if you bring it into the country) and you do not need to claim the remittance basis or complete a tax return.

Although your overseas income must be 'subject to tax' overseas, it is not necessary to have actually paid any tax on the income. Thanks to overseas personal allowances you might not be required to actually pay any tax on your overseas income. However, such income would still be considered to be 'subject to tax'.

Chapter 30

Pros and Cons of Claiming the Remittance Basis

Most UK residents are taxed on the arising basis. This means they pay UK tax on their worldwide income and capital gains.

Those who are not domiciled in the UK and have foreign income and capital gains can use the remittance basis which means they only pay tax on their overseas income and gains if and when they bring them into the UK (i.e. remit them).

From 6 April 2017, once a non-domiciled individual has been UK resident for 15 out of the last 20 tax years, they become "deemed UK domiciled" which means they can no longer use the remittance basis.

If you qualify to use the remittance basis (and are not entitled to use one of the concessions outlined in the previous chapter) you have to claim it on your tax return. If you don't, you'll be taxed on the arising basis.

Those who qualify can claim the remittance basis year by year. In other words, in some years you can claim the remittance basis, in others you can let yourself be taxed on the arising basis. This may allow you to do some constructive tax planning.

So why don't all non-doms with overseas income and capital gains, who qualify to use the remittance basis, do so all the time? Because there are two hefty penalties for using it:

- You will lose your personal allowance and CGT exemption
- You may have to pay the remittance basis charge (RBC)

All non-doms who claim the remittance basis lose their personal allowance and CGT exemption. The remittance basis charge is only payable after you've lived in the UK for a certain length of time (roughly speaking, 7 tax years). Those who arrive in the UK can therefore enjoy a short honeymoon period when they don't have to pay the charge.

It is worth remembering that the remittance basis will sometimes only *defer* UK tax, not avoid it altogether. Tax may be payable if you bring the money into the UK at a later date while you are still UK resident. It will often only be worth claiming the remittance basis if:

- The overseas income and gains are to remain overseas permanently
- You will become non-resident before the funds are remitted, or
- The funds can be remitted tax free

It's also important to point out that you may not be able to escape tax altogether by claiming the remittance basis if your overseas income and capital gains are taxed in another country. The remittance basis is most useful to those who keep their investments in tax havens or countries that have lower tax rates than the UK.

Losing Your Personal Allowance & CGT Exemption

If you claim the remittance basis you will lose various tax allowances and exemptions, the most important ones being the:

- Income tax personal allowance, and
- Capital gains tax annual exemption

For the 2017/18 tax year your personal allowance shelters the first £11,500 of your income from tax and the capital gains tax exemption shelters the first £11,300 of your capital gains from tax.

This penalty applies to all non-doms who claim the remittance basis, no matter how long they've lived in the UK.

However, if you hold dual residence status you may also qualify for a personal allowance under a double tax agreement. This means that some individuals will not lose their personal allowance by making a remittance basis claim.

To qualify you would need to be UK resident and treaty resident in one of the following countries: Austria, Barbados, Belgium, Fiji,

Ireland, Kenya, Luxembourg, Mauritius, Namibia, Netherlands, Portugal, Swaziland, Sweden, Switzerland and Zambia.

If an individual is a resident but not a citizen of Austria, Belgium, Kenya, Luxembourg, Mauritius, Portugal, Sweden, Switzerland or Zambia, they are not entitled to personal allowances if their UK income consists solely of dividends or royalties or any combination of them.

However, these individuals would need to consider whether it actually makes sense to claim the remittance basis because the other country may tax the overseas income and gains not remitted to the UK.

The main drawback for most non doms is the loss of the £11,500 income tax personal allowance. Claiming the remittance basis may save you tax on your overseas income but you could pay an extra £4,600 in UK income tax if you are a higher-rate taxpayer:

$$£11,500 \times 40\% = £4,600$$

If you have also sold residential property you could pay an extra £3,164 in capital gains tax if you lose your annual CGT exemption. That's because:

$$£11,300 \times 28\% = £3,164$$

If you've sold other assets such as shares or commercial property the top capital gains tax rate is 20%, so losing you annual CGT exemption could cost you £2,260.

The total potential tax cost from losing your personal allowance and CGT exemption is therefore £7,764 (£4,600 + £3,164).

It's important to point out that all UK taxpayers with income over £100,000 have their personal allowances gradually taken away. For 2017/18 once your income reaches £123,000 your personal allowance will have been completely withdrawn. Thus non doms with income over £123,000 have less to lose from claiming the remittance basis.

Example

Kathy is non-domiciled and has only lived in the UK for a few years (she doesn't have to pay the remittance basis charge). She has UK income of £75,000 and overseas rental income of £25,000. If she pays tax on the arising basis she will pay £10,000 tax on her overseas rental income:

$$£25,000 \times 40\% = £10,000$$

If she claims the remittance basis her overseas rental income will be tax free but she will lose her personal allowance which means her UK tax bill will increase by £4,600. Thus her overall tax saving is £5,400:

$$£10,000 \text{ tax saving} - £4,600 \text{ tax increase} = £5,400$$

If Kathy's overseas rental income was £11,500 or less she would not save any tax by claiming the remittance basis: losing her personal allowance cancels out any tax saving on her overseas income.

If Kathy was a high earner with UK income of, say £150,000, her potential tax saving could be £11,250:

$$£25,000 \times 45\% = £11,250$$

She would not lose her personal allowance by claiming the remittance basis because she doesn't qualify for one anyway (her income is over the £123,000 threshold).

Kathy's final tax saving may be less than £5,400 or £11,250 if she has to pay tax in the country where the property is located. This tax would normally be offset against her UK tax bill if the income was taxed in the UK.

Furthermore, in this example we have assumed that Kathy has no UK capital gains. If she does then claiming the remittance basis will increase her UK tax bill by up to £3,164. This is because the first £11,300 of her UK capital gains will no longer be tax free and will instead be taxed at up to 28%.

Finally, she may eventually end up paying UK tax on her overseas rental income if she brings the money into the UK at a later date. However, she won't be able to get back the personal allowance or CGT exemption she lost when she claimed the remittance basis.

These are lost forever, so she could end up paying much more tax than she would have under the arising basis.

Example continued

A few years later Kathy decides to bring the same £25,000 of overseas rental income into the UK. As a higher-rate taxpayer she will pay 40% tax – £10,000. But she won't be able to recover the personal allowance she lost when she claimed the remittance basis.

Losing her personal allowance increased her UK tax bill by £4,600 at the time. So you could say she has now paid a total of £14,600 on her £25,000 overseas rental income (£10,000 plus £4,600). In this case claiming the remittance basis has cost her dear and her overall tax rate is 58%.

Of course, if Kathy can keep her money overseas permanently then she will not face this problem. But not everyone can afford to tie their money up like this. If you intend to live in the UK for many years and have large financial commitments then it may be difficult to keep your money trapped overseas permanently.

Of course, if your overseas income is much larger than Kathy's, you may have little to lose by claiming the remittance basis. If the loss of your personal allowance and CGT exemption is tiny compared with the tax you will save, then claiming the remittance basis is probably the best thing to do.

Using the Remittance Basis to Avoid Capital Gains Tax

The remittance basis can also be used to avoid capital gains tax when you sell overseas assets:

Example

Connie is non-domiciled and has only lived in the UK for a few years (she doesn't have to pay the remittance basis charge). She is a higher-rate taxpayer which means she pays capital gains tax at up to 28%.

She sells her overseas holiday home in 2017/18 and realizes a capital gain of £100,000. She has no UK capital gains. If she pays tax on the arising basis she will pay £24,836 in capital gains tax when she sells her overseas home:

$$(£100,000 - £11,300) \times 28\% = £24,836$$

If she claims the remittance basis her overseas capital gain will be tax free but she will lose her personal allowance which means her UK tax bill will increase by £4,600. Thus her overall tax saving is £20,236:

$$£24,836 \text{ tax saving} - £4,600 \text{ tax increase} = £20,236$$

If Connie's overseas capital gain is £27,729 or less she would not save any tax by claiming the remittance basis: losing her personal allowance will cancel out any capital gains tax saving.

If Connie is a high earner with income over £123,000 she will not lose her personal allowance by claiming the remittance basis because she doesn't qualify for one anyway, so claiming the remittance basis may still be worthwhile if her overseas capital gain is smaller.

Connie's final tax saving may be less than £20,236 if she has to pay capital gains tax in the country where the property is located. This tax would normally be offset against her UK tax bill if the gain was taxed in the UK.

Furthermore in this example we have assumed that Connie has no UK capital gains. If she does then claiming the remittance basis will increase her UK tax bill by up to £3,164.

Finally, she may eventually end up paying UK capital gains tax if she brings the money into the UK at a later date.

As can be seen from the above examples claiming the remittance basis can save you tax if you are non-UK domiciled but there are traps to look out for.

In particular, it is essential to find out how much tax, if any, will be paid overseas and whether you can keep the money offshore and out of the UK taxman's clutches permanently.

The £30,000 or £60,000 Remittance Basis Charge

The second drawback of claiming the remittance basis is the annual £30,000 or £60,000 remittance charge. This charge is only payable if you've been UK resident for a certain length of time:

- £30,000 UK resident for 7 of the previous 9 tax years

- £60,000 UK resident for 12 of the previous 14 tax years

Once you've been UK resident for 15 of the past 20 tax years you become deemed UK domiciled and can no longer claim the remittance basis.

The remittance basis charge is essentially a prepayment of income tax or capital gains tax. This means it can qualify for double tax relief under many of the UK's double tax treaties.

For most taxpayers the remittance basis charge is far too heavy a price to pay. Only those with sizeable overseas income or capital gains will benefit from claiming the remittance basis. Remember that you pay this charge in addition to losing your income tax personal allowance and annual CGT exemption.

Those who stand to benefit most from making a remittance basis claim are additional rate taxpayers (those with income over £150,000). They pay income tax at 45% and capital gains tax at 28% and don't benefit from a personal allowance anyway.

However, claiming the remittance basis will only be advantageous if they also have significant amounts of overseas income and/or capital gains and the amount of tax payable on the arising basis would exceed the additional tax charges.

You can avoid the remittance basis charge by simply paying UK income tax and capital gains tax on your overseas income and capital gains under the arising basis like everyone else.

The remittance basis charge only rears its head if you've been UK resident for at least 7 of the previous 9 tax years. This gives foreign nationals who have recently arrived in the UK a 7 year 'honeymoon' period in which to claim the remittance basis without having to pay the £30,000 tax charge (although they will still lose their various tax allowances).

Example

Daniela is non-domiciled and came to the UK in 2013 to work. She wants to claim the remittance basis during the 2017/18 tax year. Looking back over the <u>previous</u> nine tax years her residence status is as follows:

1.	2008/09	*Non-resident*
2.	2009/10	*Non-resident*
3.	2010/11	*Non-resident*
4.	2011/12	*Non-resident*
5.	2012/13	*Non-resident*
6.	2013/14	*UK resident*
7.	2014/15	*UK resident*
8.	2015/16	*UK resident*
9.	2016/17	*UK resident*

Daniela was UK resident in only four out of the previous nine tax years and is therefore not subject to the £30,000 remittance basis charge.

Example revisited

Let's move forward a few years. It's the 2020/21 tax year and Daniela wants to claim the remittance basis. Looking back over the previous nine tax years her residence status is as follows:

1.	2011/12	*Non-resident*
2.	2012/13	*Non-resident*
3.	2013/14	*UK resident*
4.	2014/15	*UK resident*
5.	2015/16	*UK resident*
6.	2016/17	*UK resident*
7.	2017/18	*UK resident*
8.	2018/19	*UK resident*
9.	2019/20	*UK resident*

Daniela was UK resident in seven out of the previous nine tax years and is therefore subject to the £30,000 remittance basis charge if she decides to be taxed on the remittance basis in 2020/21.

Daniela will be subject to the £30,000 for a further five tax years. After that the remittance basis charge increases to £60,000.

Example revisited again

Let's move forward a further five years. It's the 2025/26 tax year and Daniela wants to claim the remittance basis. Looking back over the previous 14 tax years her residence status is as follows:

1.	2011/12	Non-resident	
2.	2012/13	Non-resident	
3.	2013/14	UK resident	
4.	2014/15	UK resident	
5.	2015/16	UK resident	
6.	2016/17	UK resident	
7.	2017/18	UK resident	
8.	2018/19	UK resident	
9.	2019/20	UK resident	
10.	2020/21	UK resident	£30,000 charge
11.	2021/22	UK resident	£30,000 charge
12.	2022/23	UK resident	£30,000 charge
13.	2023/24	UK resident	£30,000 charge
14.	2024/25	UK resident	£30,000 charge

Daniela was UK resident in 12 out of the previous 14 tax years and is therefore subject to the £60,000 remittance basis charge if she decides to be taxed on the remittance basis in 2025/26.

Note, the years of UK residence do not have to be consecutive:

Example

Shira is non-domiciled. It's the 2025/26 tax year and she wants to claim the remittance basis. Her residence status is as follows:

1.	2011/12	UK resident
2.	2012/13	UK resident
3.	2013/14	UK resident
4.	2014/15	UK resident
5.	2015/16	UK resident
6.	2016/17	Non-resident
7.	2017/18	Non-resident
8.	2018/19	UK resident
9.	2019/20	UK resident
10.	2020/21	UK resident
11.	2021/22	UK resident
12.	2022/23	UK resident
13.	2023/24	UK resident
14.	2024/25	UK resident

Like Daniela, Shira was UK resident in 12 out of the previous 14 tax years. The difference is that she was non-resident for a couple of years in the middle. Shira is therefore subject to the £60,000 remittance basis charge if she decides to be taxed on the remittance basis in 2025/26.

Is it Worth Paying the Remittance Basis Charge?

There are only around 5,000 people who are prepared pay the remittance basis charge. If you have millions of pounds of overseas income (or even hundreds of thousands of pounds) then £30,000 or £60,000 is probably peanuts.

However, the simple truth is that the vast majority of non-domiciled individuals do not have enough overseas income or capital gains to justify paying the remittance basis charge.

The £30,000 Remittance Basis Charge

If you've been UK resident for at least 7 of the previous 9 tax years you are subject to the £30,000 remittance basis charge. It's only worth paying this charge if it's less than your normal UK tax.

For example, if you have overseas income of £75,000, your UK income tax would normally be £30,000 if you are a higher-rate taxpayer:

$$£75,000 \times 40\% \text{ tax} = £30,000$$

So your overseas income has to be *higher* than this to make paying the £30,000 charge worthwhile.

Furthermore, if you claim the remittance basis you also have to factor in the loss of your annual CGT exemption and income tax personal allowance (although you may not qualify for a personal allowance under the arising basis either if your total income exceeds £123,000).

If you are an additional rate taxpayer (income over £150,000) your overseas income must *exceed* £66,667 before claiming the remittance basis becomes an option:

$$£66,667 \times 45\% = £30,000$$

Additional rate taxpayers don't have to worry about losing their income tax personal allowances (because they don't get one anyway) but may have to factor in the loss of their CGT exemption.

The £60,000 Remittance Basis Charge

If you've been UK resident for at least 12 of the previous 14 tax years you are subject to the £60,000 remittance basis charge.

If you are an additional-rate taxpayer (income over £150,000) your overseas income must *exceed* £133,333 before claiming the remittance basis becomes an option:

$$£133,333 \times 45\% = £60,000$$

You may also have to factor in the loss of your CGT exemption.

If you are not an additional-rate taxpayer you will be paying tax at a lower rate and therefore need *more than* £133,333 in overseas income to justify paying a £60,000 charge.

Capital Gains Tax

Some non-domiciled individuals, who wouldn't normally use the remittance basis, may use it sporadically, for example in years when large overseas capital gains are realized.

If your overseas capital gains are quite small it's probably not worth claiming the remittance basis to avoid UK capital gains tax.

If your gains for the year are less than the annual CGT exemption they can be remitted back to the UK tax free – as long as you don't have any other UK gains that have used up your exemption already. A married couple can currently enjoy £22,600 of tax-free capital gains.

Provided your other overseas unremitted income and gains are less than £2,000 there will be no further tax to pay.

If your overseas capital gains are slightly higher than the annual CGT exemption, it may still be better to pay tax on the arising basis so that you can keep your income tax personal allowance.

If you are subject to the £30,000 remittance basis charge and assuming you have no other overseas income and are a higher-rate or additional-rate taxpayer, you would need a capital gain of more than £107,143 to make claiming the remittance basis worthwhile:

$$£107,143 \times 28\% = £30,000$$

(Note, I'm assuming the gain is from *residential* property, other capital gains are taxed at lower rates.)

Similarly, if you are subject to the £60,000 charge, you would need a gain of at least £214,286 to make claiming the remittance basis worthwhile.

This ignores the loss of your annual CGT exemption from claiming the remittance basis. Taking this into account, you would need an overseas unremitted capital gain of more than £118,443 (£107,143 + £11,300) for the 2017/18 tax year, if you were subject to the £30,000 charge to justify claiming the remittance basis (£225,586 if you are subject to the £60,000 charge).

This also ignores the loss of your £11,500 personal allowance from claiming the remittance basis (assuming your income does not exceed £100,000, the point at which all UK taxpayers start to see their personal allowances withdrawn).

The personal allowance saves a higher-rate taxpayer £4,600 in income tax during the 2017/18 tax year. To compensate for the loss of this allowance you would need to have an additional £16,429 of capital gains from overseas residential property that you can shelter from UK tax by claiming the remittance basis:

$$£16,429 \times 28\% = £4,600$$

In total, you need to have at least £134,872 of unremitted capital gains before claiming the remittance basis could be worthwhile if you were subject to the £30,000 remittance basis charge:

$$£107,143 + £11,300 + £16,429 = £134,872$$

If you have to pay the £60,000 charge you need to have at least £242,015 of unremitted overseas capital gains before claiming the remittance basis makes any sense.

In the above calculations I've assumed the capital gains are all taxed at 28%. Some of your gains may, in fact, be taxed at just 18% under the arising basis if you are a basic-rate taxpayer.

Gains from assets like shares and commercial property are taxed less heavily than residential property. Higher-rate taxpayers pay 20% on their gains and basic-rate taxpayers pay 10%.

Other capital gains (e.g. from selling a business) may qualify for Entrepreneurs Relief and would be taxed at just 10% under the arising basis. In this situation, you may need overseas capital gains in excess of £300,000 (£300,000 x 10% = £30,000) before claiming the remittance basis starts to make sense.

Finally, it should be noted that many non-doms will have varying amounts of UK income and capital gains and overseas income and capital gains. Deciding whether to claim the remittance basis or not may involve some complex calculations and professional advice is recommended.

It's also important to remember the overseas tax position at this point. If the overseas capital gains tax is more than the UK tax, it would probably make sense to simply pay tax on the arising basis and let double tax relief eliminate the UK tax charge.

How to Avoid the Remittance Basis Charge

Non-UK domiciled individuals can reduce the impact of the charges levied for claiming the remittance basis in a number of ways.

You can potentially avoid paying any remittance basis charge by making sure you are non-UK resident for three years out of every ten.

In practice, however, this may be difficult to achieve.

Those who are in their seventh year of UK residence might wish to consider realising capital gains on some of their overseas assets before the £30,000 charge comes into force.

When realising capital gains on overseas assets for UK tax planning purposes, it is essential to take any potential overseas tax into account.

If you have been living in the UK for many years and are subject to the remittance basis charge, it may be worth making sure that several of your overseas capital gains fall into the same tax year. This way, UK capital gains tax can be avoided on all of your disposals for the price of one £30,000 or £60,000 charge rather than several.

Married Couples

Where a couple are both UK resident but non-UK domiciled, it may make sense to transfer all or most of their overseas assets to one of them. UK tax can then be avoided on unremitted overseas income and capital gains for the price of just one lost personal allowance, capital gains tax exemption and £30,000 or £60,000 charge, if applicable.

In some cases, it may also make sense for the couple's overseas assets to be transferred to the one who has been UK resident for the shortest amount of time. This will delay the impact of the £30,000 or £60,000 charge for as long as possible.

Managing the Remittance Basis Charge

If you have enough overseas income or capital gains to justify paying the £30,000 or £60,000 remittance basis charge, you can probably afford to pay a tax advisor to complete your tax return, keep a record of your overseas income and capital gains and help you bring your money into the UK in the most tax efficient way possible.

If you keep all of your overseas income and capital gains offshore permanently your tax position is relatively straightforward. However, if you start bringing money into the UK and remit the 'wrong' money, you may fall foul of a set of strict ordering rules that ignore the nature of what is remitted (capital gains or income) and treat the remittance in the least tax-efficient manner possible. These rules can be avoided with some careful tax planning.

Finally, if your income or capital gains are large enough to warrant paying the remittance basis charge, it's important to remember that the remittance basis can only be used for a limited number of years.

Once you have been UK resident for 15 out of the previous 20 tax years you will become deemed UK domiciled for tax purposes and will have to pay income tax and capital gains tax on the arising basis.

Chapter 31

Non Domiciled with Employment Income

If you are UK resident but non-UK domiciled your employment income may be taxable on the remittance basis if:

- You have a foreign employer
- Your employment duties are performed wholly overseas

A foreign employer is a non-resident employer.

This is an attractive tax break for non-domiciled individuals who work in countries that do not tax their employment income or tax it at a low rate.

It is acceptable to do some work in the UK but only if it is 'merely incidental' to your overseas duties. Duties performed in the UK that are of the same type as those performed overseas are not merely incidental, even if performed for a very short time.

Many non-domiciled individuals living in the UK have in the past used dual contracts to keep some of their employment income out of the UK tax net. Under a dual contract arrangement the individual would be employed by a non-resident company for his overseas duties and a UK company for his UK duties.

The UK contract would pay the individual enough income to cover living expenses while the overseas contract may allow the individual to roll up the remaining income tax free abroad and access it after becoming non-UK resident.

HMRC has never liked these arrangements, suspecting that most non-domiciled individuals would artificially split their income from related employers in two: a taxable UK part and a tax-free overseas part.

Measures have been taken to prevent non-domiciled employees from avoiding tax by artificially splitting their UK and foreign earnings using dual contracts.

Employment income from a foreign employer where the duties are performed wholly outside the UK will not be eligible for the remittance basis (and will therefore be taxed as it arises) if:

- The employee also has a UK employment (i.e. a job where duties are performed only in the UK or partly in the UK)

- The UK employer and the foreign employer are the same or associated with each another. Generally speaking, employers are 'associated' if one is controlled by the other or they are under common control

- The UK and foreign jobs are 'related', and

- The foreign tax rate on the overseas income is less than 65% of the 45% additional rate (i.e. less than 29.25%).

It may be possible to use dual contracts that are not motivated by tax avoidance (e.g. for legal or regulatory reasons).

Related Employments

A contentious issue is likely to be whether the two jobs are 'related'. Some examples of scenarios in which HMRC would consider a UK and overseas job to be related to one another include:

- Where it is reasonable to suppose the UK employment would end if the foreign employment ended

- Where the individual does the same type of work under each contract, except in different locations

- Where the two jobs involve the same customers/clients

- Where the employee is a director of either employer, or is a senior employee or one of the highest earning employees of either employer

These examples are not exhaustive and HMRC may argue that two jobs are related in other circumstances.

Non-domiciled employees who only work abroad in a genuine

foreign employment and elect the remittance basis should continue to remain exempt from UK income tax on their foreign earnings.

Where the individual has UK and overseas jobs, if he can show that the overseas job is different and that the foreign employer is not closely linked with the UK employer it may be possible to continue successfully using two contracts. However, it is possible that any such arrangement will be closely scrutinized by HMRC.

Overseas Workday Relief

Non-domiciled individuals who have not been UK resident in the three previous tax years can use the remittance basis to avoid paying UK tax on their overseas earnings.

This is known as Overseas Workday Relief and it's available for the first three tax years of UK residence.

It is possible to benefit from this relief even if some of your employment duties are performed in the UK, as long as your employer is non-resident.

Your earnings will be divided into a UK and overseas part. The part related to UK work will be taxed in the UK but the part related to overseas work is only taxed when the money is brought into the UK.

Chapter 32

Tax-Free Remittances

In some cases money or assets brought into the UK will not be treated as taxable remittances:

Remittances to Pay the £30,000 or £60,000 Charge

If you claim the remittance basis and are subject to the £30,000 or £60,000 tax charge you can remit £30,000/£60,000 to pay the charge without that money itself being treated as a taxable remittance.

The payment has to be made direct to HMRC from an overseas bank account. If the funds are paid into your own UK bank account first, this would be classed as a taxable remittance.

Clothing, Footwear, Jewellery and Watches

This is a potentially useful exemption. Clothing, footwear, jewellery and watches purchased out of foreign income and capital gains are exempt if they are for the personal use of the non-domiciled individual, his spouse or partner and children and grandchildren under 18.

These means these assets can be brought into the UK without triggering a tax charge.

Example

During an overseas trip James, a non-domiciled remittance basis user, uses his overseas income to buy four designer watches costing £5,000 each for himself, his wife and two children (who are under 18).

The watches are paid for using James's overseas income but because they are owned and used by 'relevant persons' (James and his family) they are exempt property under the personal use rule. Thus, James does not make a taxable remittance when he brings the watches into the UK.

Property Costing Less than £1,000

Apart from the exemption for clothing, footwear, jewellery and watches, any property with a value of less than £1,000 can be brought into the UK tax free. There is no requirement that the asset must be for personal use.

'Property' does not include cash. For example, if you bring cash of £999 into the UK you cannot take advantage of the £1,000 exemption.

There are provisions to prevent assets from being artificially split.

Example

Whilst on holiday Arnold, a remittance basis user, uses his foreign income to buy a fountain pen costing £500, a new laptop costing £800, a briefcase costing £300 and a camera costing £600. All of the items are brought back into the UK.

Because each item cost less than £1,000, the pen, laptop, briefcase and camera are regarded as exempt property. Thus Arnold has not made a taxable remittance.

The total cost of all the items is £2,200. However the £1,000 exemption limit applies to each item of property, unless it forms part of a set.

Property Repairs

Property isn't classed as remitted if it is only brought into the UK to be repaired or restored and is taken out again afterwards.

Temporary Importation of Property

Property that is brought into the UK temporarily will also not be classed as remitted. To qualify it needs to be here for a total of 275 or fewer qualifying days. Note that those 275 days are the maximum number of days the property can ever be in the UK, not the number of days allowed each year.

Property Placed on Public Display

Property can be brought into the UK for public display at approved museums and galleries for up to two years without triggering a taxable remittance.

Sales or Gifts of Exempt Property

Where exempt property is sold the proceeds must generally be taken offshore within 45 days. Otherwise a taxable remittance will be triggered. The asset must not be sold to another relevant person and the sale must be made on commercial arm's length terms.

If an expensive piece of jewellery is brought into the UK and given to a 17 year old daughter, this will not trigger a taxable remittance. However, when the daughter turns 18 she will cease to be a relevant person and a tax charge may result.

Business Investment Relief

Non-domiciled individuals can bring an unlimited amount of money into the UK to invest in certain businesses without triggering a taxable remittance.

The investor may be taxed on either the arising basis or the remittance basis in the tax year in which the investment is made and still benefit from the relief.

The investment must be made within 45 days of the money being brought into the UK.

The relief is claimed when you submit your tax return.

Various changes have been made to make the relief more attractive and apply from 6 April 2017.

For example, a qualifying investment used to be made by obtaining newly issued shares in a company or making a loan. From 6 April 2017, buying existing shares already in issue from another shareholder will qualify for the relief.

The company must be an eligible trading company or stakeholder company (a company investing in trading companies) or, from 6 April 2017, a "hybrid company".

The period during which eligible companies must start trading or holding investments has increased from two years to five years.

Carrying on a trade must be all the company does or substantially all it does. Where carrying on a commercial trade accounts for at least 80% of a company's total activities, the company will generally be regarded as meeting this requirement.

The company must not be listed on a recognised stock exchange.

For the purposes of this relief the term trade includes businesses that generate income from letting property, including residential property.

The term trade also covers a company involved in research and development that it hopes will lead to a commercial trade.

The term 'commercial' means with a view to making profits.

There are also some tough anti-avoidance rules whereby an investor will have his investment taxed as a remittance when any benefit is received that can be directly or indirectly attributed to the investment.

Chapter 33

Inheritance Tax Planning

When it comes to UK inheritance tax your residence status generally isn't important. It's your domicile that matters and the location of your assets.

If you are UK domiciled you will be subject to UK inheritance tax on your *worldwide* assets, even if you are non-resident.

If you are non-domiciled, your UK assets will still be subject to inheritance tax. However, your overseas assets are "excluded property" and are not subject to inheritance tax.

Example

Maria lives in the UK but is non-UK domiciled. She owns a number of properties in France, Spain and the UK and a bank account in Switzerland. If Maria dies inheritance tax will only be payable on her UK properties. Her overseas properties and bank account are excluded property for inheritance tax purposes.

Although UK assets are subject to inheritance tax if you are non-domiciled it is worth mentioning that it's relatively easy to convert many UK assets into overseas assets. There is generally no minimum time period that overseas assets have to be held to be treated as excluded property.

This means that non-domiciled individuals can, prior to death, transfer cash and other liquid assets into overseas accounts to escape inheritance tax.

Deemed Domicile

Even if you are non-UK domiciled under general principles, you will eventually become deemed UK domiciled (for income tax, capital gains tax and inheritance tax purposes).

From 6 April 2017 you will be deemed UK domiciled if you have been UK resident for at least 15 of the past 20 tax years.

You will therefore generally be treated as deemed UK domiciled at the beginning of the 16th year of UK tax residence within any 20 year period.

However, there is a concession that allows people who leave the UK to lose their deemed UK domiciled status. A person who would otherwise satisfy the test will no longer be deemed UK domiciled if they are non-resident for the tax year in question and were non-resident for the previous three consecutive tax years.

However, if they become UK resident again in years four, five or six, they will be deemed UK domiciled under the 15/20 years rule.

Thanks to the deemed domicile rule, people who come to live in the UK for many years will eventually end up subject to inheritance tax in the same way as most other UK taxpayers.

Those who are born in the UK but are nevertheless non-UK domiciled (for example, because their father is non-UK domiciled) will become deemed UK domiciled before they are adults.

An individual who is born in the UK with a UK domicile of origin but has acquired a domicile of choice in another country will be treated as UK domiciled for inheritance tax purposes if they become UK resident again and have been UK resident in at least one out of the two previous tax years.

Excluded Property

If you are non-domiciled most of your UK assets will still be subject to inheritance tax. Some UK assets are exempt, however, including:

- Foreign currency bank accounts
- Authorised Unit Trusts and OEICs

Foreign Currency Bank Accounts

If you have a UK-based foreign currency bank account and are both non-UK resident and non-domiciled when you die, the account will be exempt from inheritance tax.

Lifetime transfers out of a UK-based foreign currency accounts are not exempt, however. Instead they are treated as potentially exempt transfers, which means that inheritance tax could be payable if you die within seven years of making the transfer.

One way to avoid such transfers becoming subject to inheritance tax may be to place funds in an overseas bank account before transferring money to the UK. Transfers of non-UK property by non-domiciled individuals are exempt from inheritance tax.

Foreign currency bank accounts held by an individual deemed UK domiciled for tax purposes will be treated as being located in the UK.

Authorised Unit Trusts and OEICs

Many popular investment funds these days are authorised unit trusts or open-ended investment companies (OEICs). They are excluded property for inheritance tax purposes.

This means that non-domiciled individuals can invest in the UK stock market and bond markets via unit trusts and OEICs and their assets will not be subject to inheritance tax.

Note, however, that if you become deemed UK domiciled these assets will no longer be excluded property and will be subject to inheritance tax.

The Channel Islands & Isle of Man

If you are domiciled in either the Channel Islands or the Isle of Man the following investments are excluded property:

- War savings certificates
- National Savings & Investments premium bonds
- National Savings certificates
- Deposits with the National Savings Bank
- Savings under any certified contractual savings scheme (e.g. SAYE schemes)

UK Gilts

UK Government securities or gilts issued after 29 April 1996 are excluded property if you are *non-resident*. This means that a UK domiciled individual who emigrates can avoid inheritance tax by investing in certain Government securities. Gilts issues before that date are excluded property if you are non-domiciled and non-resident.

Non-Domiciled Spouses

Generally speaking all transfers of assets to your spouse are completely exempt from inheritance tax.

Note, the spouse exemption applies only to married couples. There is no exemption for transfers to common-law partners.

However, the spouse exemption is restricted when a UK domiciled spouse transfers assets to a non-domiciled spouse.

For transfers made before 6 April 2013 the spouse exemption was limited to £55,000. For transfers made on or after 6 April 2013 the spouse exemption is limited to the nil rate band (currently £325,000).

Any transfers above these limits, either during the transferor's lifetime or on their death, are treated just like transfers made to any other person who is not your spouse.

A single limit applies for the whole of the transferor's lifetime, even if they remarry another non-domiciled person.

The limit on exempt transfers to a non-UK domiciled spouse ceases to apply if that spouse becomes deemed UK domiciled.

Example

Rosie is UK domiciled, her husband Billy is non-domiciled. In 2012, Rosie gave Billy £60,000. £55,000 is covered by the spouse exemption, the remaining £5,000 is not. In 2016 she gave him £300,000. £270,000 is covered by the spouse exemption (£325,000 - £55,000). The remaining £30,000 is not covered.

Many transfers between spouses will not reduce the spouse exemption limit, e.g. maintenance. Other transfers not covered by the spouse exemption may qualify for other inheritance tax exemptions.

Any amounts still not covered will be potentially exempt transfers and only subject to inheritance tax if the person who makes the gift dies within seven years.

When the UK domiciled spouse dies the £325,000 nil rate band is available in the usual way for transfers in excess of the spouse exemption.

This means that a UK domiciled spouse will often be able to leave up to £650,000 to a foreign domiciled spouse free from inheritance tax, providing they have not already used any of their spouse exemption.

If you have made any other chargeable transfers in the previous seven years the amount that can be left free of inheritance tax is reduced.

Transfers from a Non-Domiciled Spouse

There is no restriction on transfers in the opposite direction: from a foreign domiciled spouse to a UK domiciled spouse. This is because such transfers may result in more inheritance tax being paid. These transfers may, however, have foreign tax implications.

Transferring Assets to a Non-Resident Spouse

We know that, from 6 April 2017, a non-domiciled person becomes deemed UK domiciled when they have been resident in the UK for at least 15 out of the last 20 tax years.

We also know that the limit on exempt transfers to a non-UK domiciled spouse ceases to apply if that spouse acquires deemed UK domicile. This opens up some interesting planning ideas for married couples with mixed domicile.

Example

Jane is UK domiciled and has significant overseas assets. Her husband Paul is non-domiciled but has lived in the UK for the last 20 years and is deemed UK domiciled.

Jane can transfer all her foreign assets to Paul and the transfer will be fully exempt from inheritance tax. If Paul leaves the country he will automatically lose his deemed UK domicile after he has been non-UK resident for three tax years.

All of Jane's overseas assets, now owned by Paul, would then be free from UK inheritance tax.

Arguably Jane could have achieved the same result by emigrating but it is harder for her to lose her UK domicile. Deemed domicile is much easier to lose – you lose it automatically after becoming non-resident for a few years.

This example ignores the capital gains tax consequences which could be important. Transfers between spouses are normally exempt from capital gains tax but Jane could be subject to CGT on the transferred assets while she is UK resident.

The Opt-in Election

If you are non-domiciled and have a UK domiciled spouse you can elect to opt-in and be treated as UK domiciled for inheritance tax purposes.

The election does not change your status for income tax or capital gains tax purposes.

You're not allowed to make the election unless you have a UK domiciled spouse.

The election can be backdated by up to seven years but not to a date before 6 April 2013.

The election is irrevocable and will apply for the rest of your life – unless you become non-UK resident for a period of four consecutive tax years, in which case the election automatically ceases to apply.

Although you will be treated as UK domiciled for most inheritance tax purposes, there are some exceptions:

- Certain Government securities and other excluded property will keep that status

- The provisions of any applicable double tax treaty are unaffected

- Double tax relief will continue to be available where the person is also subject to inheritance tax in another country

Advantages and Disadvantages of the Election

The main advantage is that transfers from the UK domiciled spouse to the non-UK domiciled spouse will be completely exempt from inheritance tax. This means that other inheritance tax exemptions and allowances will not be used up making transfers to the non-UK domiciled spouse.

The main disadvantage is that all of the non-domiciled spouse's assets will be subject to inheritance tax (subject to the terms of any double tax treaty).

One option may be to set up an excluded property trust or make other transfers before the election becomes effective (see below).

Generally speaking, an opt-in election could be worth making if the UK domiciled spouse owns most of the assets. The election may not be worth making if the non-domiciled spouse has substantial foreign assets.

Excluded Property Trusts

If you are currently non-domiciled but expect to become deemed UK domiciled in the future, you can shelter your overseas assets from inheritance tax by transferring them into an excluded property trust.

Assets held in an excluded property trust will generally be exempt from UK inheritance tax if:

- The settlor (the person who establishes the trust) is non-domiciled and not deemed UK domiciled when the trust is established, and

- The assets are situated outside the UK

Any foreign assets settled into trust by previously UK domiciled individuals, while they are domiciled outside the UK, will no longer be treated as excluded property if the individual becomes UK resident again.

UK Residential Property

Non-domiciled individuals, whether UK resident or not, have only been liable to UK inheritance tax on property situated in the UK. However, once you become deemed UK domiciled both your UK and overseas assets are subject to UK inheritance tax.

For this reason it has been common practice for non-domiciled individuals who expect to become deemed UK domiciled (because they've been living in the UK for the required number of years) to place their overseas assets in an excluded property trust.

Where a non-resident trust holds overseas assets and is created by a non-domiciled individual before they become deemed UK domiciled, it will continue to be sheltered from UK inheritance tax. The assets will continue to be treated as "excluded property".

That's the good news. The bad new is the Government has decided to make UK residential property held indirectly by non doms through offshore entities (such as offshore companies and trusts) subject to inheritance tax.

It has been common practice for non-UK domiciled individuals to escape inheritance tax by holding UK residential property in an offshore company. This made it possible to escape inheritance tax because the asset in question was no longer UK property but rather shares in an overseas company. Being non-UK assets these shares were treated as "excluded property" for inheritance tax purposes. Putting the company into a trust before becoming deemed UK domiciled ensured that the excluded property status continued.

To bring these UK residential properties back into the inheritance tax net, the definition of excluded property is being changed from 6 April 2017 so that shares in offshore "close companies" and partnerships that derive their value from UK residential property will no longer be treated as excluded property. Instead they will be treated as UK assets subject to inheritance tax. (A close company is generally one owned and controlled by five or fewer people.)

The new rules will apply to non-domiciled individual shareholders and to trusts with non-domiciled settlors from 6 April 2017. The rules will apply to all chargeable events so trusts with such assets will be exposed to inheritance tax charges at ten-yearly intervals and, potentially, on the death of the settlor.

Interests of less than 1% in a close company or partnership were to be disregarded for the purposes of the new inheritance tax rules. However, in the March 2017 Budget it was announced that this limit would be increased to 5%.

A number of anti-avoidance provisions will be introduced, particularly concerning the use of debt, to counteract any artificial arrangements to reduce the net value of the taxable estate.

Where a double tax treaty gives another country the taxing rights, but that country does not actually levy inheritance tax, the new legislation will override the double tax treaty and give the UK the right to tax the asset.

A new anti-avoidance rule will also be introduced to override any arrangements whose main purpose is to avoid inheritance tax on residential property.

Sale proceeds may continue to be treated as UK residential property for a further two years.

These new rules apply to all residential properties, including rental properties. Non-domiciled individuals may still be able to benefit from holding other non-UK assets and UK commercial property in a foreign company.

Many company structures used to hold UK residential property (but usually not rental property) are subject to the Annual Tax on Enveloped Dwellings. Without the potential inheritance tax savings, many of these structures will become highly unattractive.

Double Tax Treaties

The UK has double tax treaties with the following countries in relation to inheritance tax:

- France
- Irish Republic
- India
- Italy
- Netherlands
- Pakistan
- South Africa
- Sweden
- Switzerland
- USA

These agreements normally apply if you have a connection (e.g. residence, domicile) with one of the countries.

They generally allow the country where you are domiciled to tax all your assets. The other country can tax property situated in that country.

Treaties with France, Italy, India and Pakistan were in place before 1975 during the estate duty era and have different rules. If you are domiciled in one of those countries you may be protected from UK inheritance tax on your overseas assets even if you are deemed UK domiciled. Overseas assets may, however, be taxable if there is a UK will.

Many of the tax treaties contain detailed rules concerning what assets can be taxed by each country. Most will allow the UK to tax assets like real estate situated in the UK.

If a transfer is liable to inheritance tax and also to a similar tax imposed by another country with which the UK does not have an agreement, you may be able to get relief under unilateral relief provisions.

Lightning Source UK Ltd.
Milton Keynes UK
UKOW05f0310210417
299602UK00005B/62/P